Small Town Salon Secrets

*True stories from Lisa's Classic Cuts
that will curl your hair!*

Lisa Maria, hairstylist and Anne Treimanis, Esq.

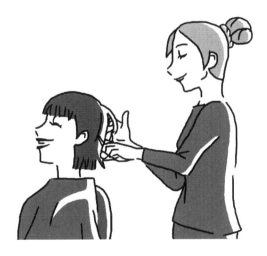

Enjoy!
Anne Treimanis

ISBN:1481146041
ISBN-13: 978-1481146043

DEDICATION

From Lisa:
This book is dedicated to my son Joey, the shining light of my life. I love you until the end of time.

I want to also give thanks and acknowledge my mother, who has supported me through all of my adventures, in and out of the salon.

Finally, I wish to give thanks to all of my clients, for whom I snip the scissors each and every day.

From Anne:
It's been so much fun to write this book with Lisa. I've enjoyed our 17 year ongoing conversation, which always took place in the salon.

I dedicate this book to my four wonderful children – Ieva, Robbie, Karl, and Erik, all of whom I love dearly. Thanks for your support and for holding on to each other during the roller coaster rides.

I want to especially thank and acknowledge the family I was born into, the unforgettable Treimanis clan! They always believed in me.

And a toast to New Canaan, Connecticut, a place we call home, where all of these adventures really took place!

From Shannon, our Editor:
This book is also for Danny and Deenna Kite and James Thomas. Everything is for you.

Cover Design: *Aria Rastandeh*

TABLE OF CONTENTS

CHAPTER 1:
29 FOREST STREET

"Hey girl, finally! It's about time you came in here." Ashley greeted Lisa with a smile as the bell tinkled and Lisa entered The Yankee Clipper Barbershop. Ashley whirled around an empty chair in front of a large mirror and invited Lisa to sit down. Lisa hopped her petite five foot four inch frame into Ashley's chair and leaned back while Ashley slung the apron around Lisa's neck and over her clothes. Ashley hauled Lisa's chair up to the sink and the young blonde who so favored Marilyn Monroe leaned back for the customary wash, eyes closed.

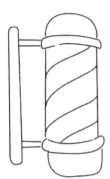

"None too soon too, I've got to leave The Yankee Clipper." Lisa's eyes opened and she looked up at Ashley.

"Why?"

"Johnny won't give me my overtime pay. I've asked him for it twice now. I'm going to start putting in applications around town." Ashley lathered up Lisa's tresses and began to massage her scalp.

"Are you going to quit outright?"

"I have no idea Lisa, but I know that I need money and if I'm going to work, he's going to pay me. Ashley sniffed and began to rinse, shaking out her own short bob. "Your hair is still so great. How far are you away from graduation?"

"I've got three more weeks until the final and I'll be licensed." Lisa attended the same styling school that Ashley had attended. Ashley had been ahead of her, and was already licensed to be a hairdresser. She wasn't bad either – Lisa had kept seeing Ashley after she had left the school, letting her practice the occasional new style or cut on her blonde hair. She was good, there was no doubt about it, but she wondered about her trouble with The Yankee Clipper.

"Where are you going to go?" Lisa closed her eyes again.

1

"There's a couple of other places here in town, we're not that small, you know." Ashley began to rinse Lisa's hair, and turned the water off. She towel dried it and sat Lisa upright, combing it so that it would be ready to cut.

"Want anything new today?" Lisa shrugged and shook her head.

"Just the usual." Ashley began cutting in Lisa's usual style, and a comfortable silence lapsed between the two women. Ashley snipped and clipped with her scissors while Lisa daydreamed there in the chair. It would happen one day; she would have her license, her own shop, and excellent stylists working for her. Lisa's client list would be a mile long, and then one day, someone huge would walk into her salon and Lisa would become famous.

"Are you even listening to me?" Lisa was snapped out of her reverie when the scissors stopped snipping and Ashley leaned over Lisa to get her attention. Lisa shook her head clear.

"What?" she asked confusedly.

"I said, are you going to Katie's party tonight?" Katie was another girl that she had been to school with, who like Ashley, had left the school with her license before Lisa.

"No," said Lisa thoughtfully. "Not really my scene."

Ashley laughed and spun Lisa around in her chair to face the mirror that was behind them.

"Perfect as usual," sighed Lisa. She got up from the seat and shook the apron off. Ashley slid around the chair and met Lisa at the register, and they chatted a little more.

"Where are you going to be next week?" Lisa asked.

"I don't know; I'll give you a call if I quit here sooner."

Ashley called Lisa the next day.

"You won't find me at The Yankee Clipper next week, Lisa."

"You found another job already?"

"Yea, I work for Orv Byron now over at Jacob's barber shop."

"That old man on Forest Street with the barber pole?"

"Yep."

"I thought he only shaved old men?"

"Do you want me to keep cutting your hair or not?"

"Ashley."

"Lisa. Look, just come down here on Friday, and check the place out. It's old, and could use a woman's touch, but it's just a barber shop. It's perfect. You'll love it. Come see me."

Lisa agreed to follow Ashley to Orv's shop in a couple of weeks. She had heard of the shop before but she had never ventured over that way. It was a month before she looked up the barber shop and went for a cut.

The shop was more than Ashley had described. It was deceptive, it was the kind of place so comfy and out of the way that you'd think it was someone's house. It had actually been a house at one time; the building had stood as a home in the 1800's, with ornate Victorian shutters and a large porch that now had a couple of chairs on it for customers to sit and wait outside the shop. Long after it had been a house, the building had been much more: it housed a Chinese laundry, a Baptist church and finally after a fire destroyed the first Jacob's Barber Shop, it was a fine establishment of hair cutting. Lisa fell in love with it immediately.

The inside was so classic looking. There were only four cutting chairs, and the place could hardly be called a "salon" - it was a true barber shop. The inside was large, with a few hair cutting chairs, and a big diamond shaped mirror to watch Orv cut hair in. Lined up against the mirror were bottles of lilac vegetal aftershave, and stacks of combs and scissors. In the corner was a checkerboard for men to huddle over and curse each other over bad moves, while they smoked cigarettes and waited for Orv to finish up a shave or a haircut. An old TV stood in the back of the barber shop, one of those monstrosities from the Sixties in the big wooden cases, with tin foiled rabbit ears to pick up the occasional baseball game. There was rarely a seat to be had unless you were having a haircut and it wasn't unusual to find people standing and waiting. And if you wanted a haircut, wait you would.

Orv didn't take appointments. Orv was good; you could tell that he had been cutting hair his entire life. There was always something going on any given day - one gentleman was in a chair with a hot towel over his face waiting for a shave, and another sat reading a magazine while Orv snipped away. Orv really could snap his scissors. Most of Orv's customers were men but a few women

3

did come in periodically.

Lisa opened the door and was greeted by dark wood walls and floor, and green marble counter tops. It was very male, and Ashley had been right, it needed a woman's touch. You could see that Ashley had been here for a couple of weeks – there were already flowers by the door on a little table and Lisa noticed that the blinds were pulled up to let the sunshine through the dusty windows. Today an old man sat snoozing alone by the checkerboard, and Ashley was cutting a client's hair while a young man swept the floor, arguing with the barber, who certainly must have been Orv.

"Dad, I don't want to cut hair, I want to be a cop." The younger man pushed the broom around and stopped to lean on it. "I've been doing this for a while, and I'm just done with it."

"Andy, I've been cutting hair all my life, it's a good job. Steady. What's wrong with it?!" Orv went over to the man sleeping in the corner and shook him by the shoulder. Motioning to the chair, the man got up from his sunlit patch and moseyed over to the empty barber chair. Lisa picked up a magazine and listened to the exchange, fascinated. Two more men walked in and went to the back of the barber shop, standing there since Lisa was taking up one of the chairs by the checkerboard.

"I've been cleaning this place up since I was a kid, and this floor never gets any balder. Listen, did you know that up in Waterbury the police train these dogs to do whatever they want? They train their dogs to find bodies, and drugs and make rescue missions." He started sweeping again. "I'm going, Dad. This place isn't for me anymore."

"This barber shop has been in this family since my dad had it over on Main Street." Ashley huffed and rolled her eyes while the man in the chair tittered from underneath a hot towel. Andrew chimed in with his father, chorusing what was obviously a well-known speech. Orv continued.

"Your grandfather Jacob was the best barber in this county. He opened up Jacob's in 1912 and it stayed right there on Main Street till the place burnt to the ground. Fifty years, in that shop before I moved it over here. Every morning, my Dad would come in at seven sharp and turn on that pole and start cuttin' hair. He cut hair

4

right up till he couldn't move his hands anymore, damned arthritis. I intend to do the same, but I guess you aren't me are you?" He looked at his son for a moment, who was gathering up the clippings and tossing them into the trash.

"No Dad, I am not." Andrew dumped the hair into the waste bucket and turned to his father, looking him in the eye. Orv stared him back, and then finally conceded to Andrew with a deep sigh.

"I don't have much of a choice, do I?"

"Nope!" came a voice from under the towel. Ashley laughed out loud and patted the man's shoulder. Andrew smiled at Orv, and Orv grabbed his hand and gave it a manly shake.

"Go on and be whatever you want son, but I've got to ask who's going to shave Jerry here if you're not going to do it." Orv turned his attention to the man in the chair, pulling the towel up and lathering him up. Andrew smiled, and exited to the backroom. The man in Ashley's chair sat up straight and ran a comb through his hair, giving himself an old fashioned pompadour style. He stood up and pulled some money out of his pocket, pressing it into Ashley's hand and kissing her on the cheek. Ashley walked over to the till, an old fashioned cash register that made a satisfying *ching!* She opened the drawer and put the money inside, scribbling a note in a ledger next to it. The man walked out and Ashley brushed the seat off for Lisa and pointed to it. The old men standing in the back positioned themselves at the checkerboard and each lit a cigarette, already talking trash to each other.

"Ashley, this place is great!" exclaimed Lisa. Ashley slung an apron around Lisa's neck.

"Ashley, who is this young lady here? Another client of yours?" Orv gave her a smile while he shaved Jerry's face, who was dozing in his chair in the same way he had been at the checkerboard.

"She's more than a client Mr. Orv; she's a hairdresser, too. We went to the same school. I believe she just got her license. "

"Is that so?" said Orv. He turned and eyed the stockroom door that Andrew had disappeared through. "School puts out pretty good hair dressers I suppose," he said, nodding at Ashley. "She came on in here and demanded I put her to work, said she was the

5

best." Ashley smiled at Lisa and winked.

Lisa leaned back and Ashley sprayed her hair with water, combing out the locks. Ashley already knew what Lisa wanted, and got to work right away. While Lisa got her hair cut, she asked questions.

"So, Mr. Orv, you've been on Forest Street since the Sixties?" Orv lit up when she asked about the shop. Jerry snorted, and Ashley huffed again.

"Y'all pipe down. Yes, I've been here since the 60s, 'bout 64, 65 I guess. We used to be over there next to an old burger joint and it burnt down and took the whole shop with it. My Dad opened up that shop in 1912, and cut hair for as long as I can remember. It was more than a living. Shakey Jake was famous in New Canaan."

"Why'd they call him Shakey Jake?" asked Lisa.

"Cause at the end of his run his hands weren't worth a damn a'tal." said Jerry. The two old men in the corner looked up from their game at the conversation.

"Best hair cut you could find in town though, even when his hands wouldn't let him." intoned the man running the black checkers across the board. The two lapsed back into cursing at each other.

"My Daddy wouldn't trust a soul else with his hair either," piped the red player. "Now we got Orv." Orv shook his head and smiled at the memory.

"Now Andy thinks he's too good to be a barber," huffed Orv. "Doesn't want to cut hair, and wants to be a police officer of all things."

"Police work isn't bad," said Jerry. "Hell, Waterbury is not bad either, and I guess he's pretty good with animals." Orv snorted.

"Said it was his 'life calling' to train dogs to sniff out bombs."

"Is not nothing wrong with helpin' out, Orv." Orv lapsed into a silence.

"He could help out around here, too." He interjected. "Who's going to help me cut hair now? It's just me and Ashley as it is, and she's bringing in customers too."

"I could help." The words were out before Lisa realized she'd said them. Ashley smiled behind her and didn't say a word, and

Jerry and Orv both looked at her. She looked back at them. "Hire me," she said confidently, and shrugged a little.

Jerry turned back but Orv's eyes lingered on her face. She smiled at him. Lisa had already felt the tug of the barber shop. It was a stop in time, and everyone knew it, even Orv. It's why he wanted to keep it the way it was.

"All right then. I guess I could use you. Come in tomorrow at 9am, we'll see what you have." Orv went back to Jerry, drawing him up and getting him ready for an around the ears trim. Ashley tapped Lisa on the shoulder in triumph. She looked over at Orv.

"You won't be disappointed," bragged Ashley of Lisa.

Turns out, he wasn't.

Lisa had been working for Orv for about seven months when one day the barber shop filled up with people. It was the busiest day that any of them had seen in a while, which was saying something, since there were people in the shop almost every day waiting for a shave and a cut. It was this day, when Orv decided that maybe it was best to hire another hairdresser.

"You girls do a lot for the business, but I think we need

another pair of hands in here," he commented as he watched men thread in and out, waiting. There were four chairs for cutting in the shop, and while there was the checkerboard, there wasn't much else. Lisa and Ashley had long built their reputation and now women were coming into the shop regularly along with the men.

"In fact," he added, "I talked to a couple of girls yesterday about coming in a couple days a week. Ashley, you'll be in charge when I'm not here, and you three can work as a team. The other girl only wants the weekends and she agreed that we could call her when she's busy. Don't think I won't be keeping an eye on you though." As they cut hair and swept up the shop that day, Lisa contemplated what the new barber would be like.

Lisa was surprised that he had already hired someone, and was again surprised by the appearance of a tall, well-built woman with sheets of blonde hair. Her name was Gabriella, and she got along well with Ashley. Gabriella was pretty, the kind of pretty that made a girl believe that everyone underneath her was "less." She wasn't snotty, but the only person that Gabriella was really into was Gabriella. One day, while Orv was out running errands, the two struck up a conversation, while Lisa just listened.

"I got this primo stuff the other day, Ashley, you should give it a try," said Gabriella. Lisa looked at Ashley – she had known Ashley was a party girl, but on drugs? Really?

"I dunno, chick, I think maybe we should wait til after work. I mean, we gotta keep it real on the job." Lisa was relieved and wanted zero to do with Gabriella. She was an average hairdresser, and had done a few color jobs that were pretty spectacular, but other than her looks, there was generally nothing fantastic about her. Ashley didn't seem to agree.

"Yea, we can get together after work though, that sounds great." Ashley changed the subject then, glancing over at Lisa from time to time while they chatted and cut hair. When the doors to the shop were locked, Ashley once again asked Lisa out with the girls.

"You sure, girl, come on, it'll be fun." Ashley begged. Lisa smiled and shook her head.

"Orv won't like it if we're late in the morning." is all she would reply. Gabriella sniffed and giggled at Ashley.

"So what? All work and no play makes Lisa a dull girl. Forget about her." She linked her arm through Ashley's and they walked to Gabriella's car. Lisa shook her head again and let them go. The next morning, Lisa could see that the party had taken it's toll on Ashley. She looked ill.

"Hit it too hard last night, Ashley?" Gabriella had called in sick today, and wasn't at the shop.

"I plead the fifth," chuckled Ashley. She did feel a little green, but wasn't going to let that take over her life. She gave some good haircuts that day, and at the end of the day, Gabriella called the shop to talk to Ashley. After a few minutes on the phone, Ashley hung up and went back to sweeping up. As Lisa was wiping down the chairs, Ashley fiddled with her purse.

"So...we're almost done." Lisa already knew where Ashley was going.

"You can go on ahead, I can finish up tonight. Take my slips and go ahead and put them in the till, and then I'll just lock up." Ashley smiled gratefully and took Lisa's tickets and put them away. Kissing Lisa on the cheek, she left the shop, looking like she had been feeling fantastic all day.

Ashley came in the next day wearing big black sunglasses and

9

wincing at the noise in the barber shop when it got busy. Gabriella didn't look any worse for the wear, although she had been 'sick' the day before. Between customers, Gabriella spent her time in the bathroom, and Ashley had taken up smoking around the side of the building. They both worked hard when Orv was in the shop, but when he was gone, Gabriella was usually nowhere to be found, and Ashley was often outside smoking. Customers had been calling in to complain, but neither Gabriella nor Ashley made any comments on any of it. Gabriella continued to call out, while Ashley came to work after what Lisa was sure were several all-nighters. She too, spent more time in the bathroom at work now.

Lisa continued to cut hair while Ashley fooled around. She remained concerned, but Ashley's work was slipping. She had given two bad haircuts this week, and Jerry had waited plenty long for his shave. Ashley was spraying down another customer's hair for a cut when Lisa saw her nodding her head out of the corner of her eye. Ashley was falling asleep. Lisa was furious.

"Hey!" Lisa barked at Ashley. Ashley's eyes snapped open and she dropped the spray bottle. "Can you please wake up?" Just then Gabriella came out of the bathroom with watering eyes and a stuffy nose. She blinked at Lisa and Ashley, looked a bit dazed. Fuming, Lisa took the bottle and scissors from Ashley and surveyed them both.

"Why don't you both just go, just go home." Lisa waved her hand at the door and stepped in front of Ashley, who swayed a little bit on the spot. Gabriella didn't waste time.

"Oh, ok, Lisa's got this, great. I'm outta here!" She gathered up her purse and keys from her station and left, the doorbell ringing merrily in her wake. Lisa widened her eyes at Ashley, as if to say "Are you going?" and Ashley shrugged.

"Who's going to lock up?" Ashley asked. Ashley was supposed to be Orv's shop manager.

"You can come back and lock up at the end of the day, just get out right this minute, ok? Don't come back to work screwed up." Lisa looked away from her. "Hey, you heard what Orv said yesterday, right? He's about to start cutting down his days to three days a week. I'm not doing this with you." Ashley sniffed and shrugged again. She gathered her stuff up and left Lisa standing there behind the customer. The customer looked up at Lisa.

"You're not going to fall asleep, are you?" Lisa smiled.

"Not today." Lisa gave him a stellar haircut, all the while fuming underneath her pretty white smile. The day wore on and Lisa cut hair, swept the floor, shaved Jerry and loaded the till. Finally, as the clock wore down to 8pm, Ashley came rolling in. She looked fresh from the shower and was dressed to kill.

"Where are you going tonight, Ashley?" Lisa asked innocently.

"We're hitting the Cove tonight." Ashley didn't look at her. She was busy separating hair cutting slips into piles. Lisa noticed what she was doing.

"Hey, I think that one's in the wrong pile." Lisa noticed that a slip in her hand writing had made it into Ashley's pile that she had reserved for her. Ashley pulled it out and smiled.

"Thanks, girl, you really look out for a friend." Ashley finished counting the slips and took the money to Orv's office, putting it in the locked box that he had in his office. He would make the deposit in the morning after Lisa got there, although Lisa had begged him to get a safe. Orv had said that he felt safe. Ashley waited for Lisa to get her things and they walked out of the shop together. It went on like that for a while. Ashley would often leave the shop to Lisa in the early afternoon when it got slow, and come back later when the shop was closed. Gabriella was there once in a while, but almost never when she was being scheduled. It came to a head one Friday afternoon when Orv handed Lisa an envelope with her pay in it.

"Orv, I did more haircuts here than you're paying me for." Lisa said it matter of factly, looking Orv in the eye. "I think Ashley has been shifting the tickets."

"What do you mean," asked Orv. "They're all right here." Orv motioned to his desk at the pile of slips laying there. Lisa closed her eyes briefly.

"Orv, Gabbie and Ashley are gone almost as much as you are. If it's not Gabriella calling out, it's Ashley leaving early to go pick her up. She comes in every night and counts the tickets out. I've

11

seen her put my tickets in her and Gabriella's pile, which means that I'm not getting paid for my work. They are."

Orv looked at her for a moment and pursed his lips. "Can you prove it?"

"I can prove they aren't here. Ask your customers." Orv scowled at her.

"If you can't prove it, I can't do anything." Orv turned away. "But I'll keep a sharper eye on things." Case closed. Lisa frowned. Did Orv believe her? Lisa wasn't sure, but she knew that something had to be done. She would wait – just a bit longer, and do whatever she could until then to keep her job.

Orv made good on his promise to keep a closer eye on things. While he was still there only three days a week, he made it a point to drop in often, coming in at different hours of the day. It went on like that for a while; weeks passed with Lisa being there more often than not while the other girls left, but they had been lucky so far. Orv hadn't come in while they weren't there. One afternoon, it was just her and Ruby – the hairdresser that often pitched in when things got extra busy. Orv dropped in the shop and looked around. Ruby was prepping Jerry for his haircut, and Lisa was already wrist deep in a shampoo.

"Where's Ashley and Gabbie?" He looked around the shop scowling, arranging the barber chairs and some things on the counter as he waited for an answer. Lisa started to reply and Ruby beat her to the punch

"Gabbie had a doctor's appointment and Ashley had an emergency. Lisa just stared at Ruby. Lisa had called Ruby herself to come in – Gabriella didn't even show up and Ashley had left after a cellphone call, which Lisa was sure had been from Gabriella. Oddly, she hadn't told Ruby that Gabriella hadn't bothered to call; only that she had let Ashley go home early. Lisa didn't tell her that Gabriella had done anything. She mentioned none of this, but instead gave Orv a smile. Leaving her customer in the chair with a hot towel draped over his face, she picked up her tickets and separated them from the ones that Ruby had placed on the spike by the ledger and the old fashioned till.

"Here's the haircuts I did today Orv." Orv took her slips and

12

counted them. He gave her a shrewd look, and dismissed her. She had made her point, and Orv had seen it, but Lisa knew that without hard evidence, Orv wasn't going to change the way he ran things. He did a once around the shop, checking and counting things. He walked over to the old TV and slapped the top of it.

"I was thinking about replacing this old thing." he said, switching it on. It was big, old – and black and white. Orv's father had brought it from his house when he opened up the shop here. The rabbit ears were bent and they were covered in foil. Ruby looked up from her haircut and agreed.

"None too soon, Mr. Orv, that thing is ancient!" Lisa was quiet still. Orv switched the TV off and waved a hand at it. "Maybe next week," he muttered. Orv finished fiddling around and left the shop. Ashley came in as usual and locked up the shop, and Lisa went home troubled. She didn't want to leave Orv, he was a great boss. But Ashley and Gabriella were leaving her the work and Ruby knew a little too much about what they were up to. None of it added up, but Lisa knew that it couldn't continue. Ashley had plenty of clients that had followed her, and while Gabriella didn't have a whole lot of unique skill, she was popular with the men, and they came in expecting to see her. What they usually got was Lisa, overwhelmed and in a hurry because neither Ashley nor Gabriella were around. Most of all, Ashley and Gabriella were still getting paid for work they weren't doing. Ridiculous. That night, as she lay in bed reading a book, Orv called her cell phone. It wasn't too late – it was before midnight, but it was late enough for concern.

"Is everything alright?" she asked Orv concerned. "Are *you* alright?" Orv huffed on the other end. He was calling from the shop.

"Yes, I'm fine," he said gruffly. "Could you come in tomorrow at seven, instead of nine? I'm going to need you there when I open the shop tomorrow."

"Sure, I guess so, Orv. Are you *sure* you're alright?" Orv didn't sound happy, and he had never called her in early before.

"I'm fine already. See you in the morning." He hung up the phone, and she flipped her cell phone closed, and turned off the light, falling asleep quickly.

13

Lisa woke in the morning, and got to the shop at seven. Gabriella and Ashley were already there, and so was Orv. He hadn't turned on the pole, which was unusual. She noticed that the TV from the corner was gone, and had been replaced by a modern color television on a stand. There were two or three chairs around it; now that the big rabbit eared box was gone, there was more room in the corner. Orv had brought it in last night. He motioned for the women to come into his office and he sat behind his desk with his fingers laced together.

"Does anyone have anything they want to tell me?" He tapped his fingers on the desk. Lisa sat in the extra chair and fiddled with her purse, looking at Gabriella and Ashley. Ashley shrugged, and Gabriella shook her head. They looked at each other. Orv opened his desk drawer and reached inside, shuffling some things around. He pulled out a silver foil packet. Ashley's eyes grew big and Lisa's brow furrowed. Gabriella looked calm, but the coppery odor of fear enveloped the room, and a fine sheen of sweat broke out on her forehead.

"Who does this belong to?" He opened the package, and shook the white powder into the trash. "Looks like cocaine, awfully expensive stash," he said to the silent women. He looked at each of them in turn. Gabriella watched dolefully as he dumped the cocaine into the trash. Ashley was staring straight ahead, jogging her leg up and down. Lisa looked him in his eye, and lifted her chin.

"Not me," she said. "I don't do drugs." Ashley came to life just then.

"It's not mine either, I'm clean." Ashley's voice wavered, and Gabriella threw her hands up.

"Well it's certainly not mine, where did it even come from?" She had an attitude, and she glared at Orv and Lisa, but kept her composure intact. Orv got up from his desk and paced behind it, upset.

"I found it last night when I was moving the TV. It was hidden in the foil of the rabbit ears, blended right in. If I hadn't moved the TV, I'd have never found it. I opened it up, and there it was." Ashley shook her head.

"That's astonishing," she said. "Maybe it belongs to one of the clients that come in and watch the TV. We can't be on top of them all the time." Gabriella fell into Ashley's excuses.

"Yea, we've been getting some different clients in here lately, too." She studied her nails. "New people," she added, as if that settled things. Orv looked at Lisa. Lisa shook her head. Orv put his palms on the desk and leaned on it.

"I won't have this. In all my years as a barber, I've never had an issue like this, not even in the Sixties. I won't have drugs in my shop, and if I find out this belongs to one of you, you're all out of here. Lisa started to protest but thought better of it; her mouth hung open for a moment and she closed it back. Ashley and Gabriella exchanged a glance with each other, and Orv motioned for them to leave his office.

For the rest of the day, Lisa noticed that things were tense around the barber shop. Orv didn't speak much to any of the them, and there were none of the problems that Lisa had had with the other girls in the past. That in itself was heaven. Orv stayed all day, and counted out the tickets at the end of the night. He took them to his desk, counted out the till and did all of his own duties, telling Ashley that she could go on home and that he would lock up. He didn't come in the next day, but things were returning to normal. Ashley was on time, and Gabriella stopped calling out. Unfortunately, Lisa's good luck only lasted a short week. After the drug scare blew over, it was back to the same old thing – Gabriella called out and Ashley was back to leaving early and coming back to count the tickets at night. Lisa started logging her own haircuts on a separate sheet, and writing down times that Gabriella called out or Ashley left early. One Friday, when Orv handed her another short payment, she confronted him.

"Look, I'm not saying it again, they're not coming in, and Ashley is covering their butts with my barber tickets." Lisa was furious. Orv was still skeptical.

"Lisa, I told you, if you can't prove it, there's not much I can do." Lisa pulled her own handwritten ledger from her pocket. It had all of her notes on it – Ashley left early here, and Gabriella called out this day. There was a definite difference between Lisa's ledger and the one that Ashley had kept all week. Orv scratched his chin and went back to his office, counting out the rest of Lisa's money. He called Ashley and Gabriella into his office – oh they were there on pay day, you bet! As they entered, Orv sat behind his desk once more and laced his fingers together again.

"Ashley, it seems to me that you've been fudging the books." Orv looked at her squarely and she turned rather pale. "Lisa here has been keeping up with her own tickets and they don't match up with your work." He said it matter of fact, and Lisa felt a small nugget of triumph drop to her stomach. Ashley looked aghast.

"But I don't understand, we do just as many haircuts as she does," retorted Ashley. Lisa shook her head and cut her off.

"No, you don't. You leave early almost every afternoon," Lisa exclaimed and pointed at Gabriella. "She doesn't even show up, and then *you,"* she ground out, flicking her finger at Ashley again, "come in and count the tickets at the end of the night and take half of them for yourself." Orv was watching the debate interestedly. Gabriella leaned over and looked at Lisa.

"I call when I'm not going to be here, thank you, and I always come in on time." she said.

"What, once a week? Sometimes two days in row?" Lisa could feel the roots of her hair getting warm and her face flushing with anger.

"I'm here every day that I'm supposed to be." Ashley looked at Lisa challengingly.

"How many times did you leave early this week?" Lisa couldn't contain her volume anymore. Gabriella and Ashley were going back and forth, nit picking the accusations that Lisa had placed in front of them and worse, they were sticking to their guns. When Lisa asked Gabriella a question, Ashley answered that it wasn't true, and when she spoke to Ashley, it was Gabriella that responded in kind defense of both of them. Orv watched the exchange, and Lisa was getting angrier by the second. The two of them were now barking about how great they were, but both of them had skated over the fact that they were stealing her money. Orv had apparently forgotten, too. He stood up and waved a hand impatiently at the gaggle of women arguing in his office.

"Ashley, go on out there and get the shop opened up. Gabbie, your shift isn't until three. Lisa, you can go ahead and help Ashley get started." Lisa waited until the other two left. She blocked Orv from the door.

"What are you going to do?" Orv looked at her bluntly.

"What can I do?" he said, shrugging. Lisa's eyes filled with tears.

"You can make them tell the truth!" she cried.

"You can't force the truth out of people. I just don't have the energy for it." Orv looked around. "We need the hands around the shop."

Lisa stepped aside and lifted her chin. *Not happening.*

"Well then you can take the next two weeks and find yourself a different pair of hands, because I won't be working here anymore." She pivoted and left Orv's office, grabbing her things and putting them by her station. It was a long day. It was going to be a longer two weeks.

CHAPTER 3:
THE DEATH OF LISA'S CAREER

Orv didn't say much to Lisa for the next few days, and while he acted apologetic he didn't try and deter her from quitting. Lisa, however, silently wished she'd never opened her mouth. Ashley and Gabriella were there at their regular times, and Ashley was rather negative towards Lisa. It was becoming miserable, but by Wednesday, she didn't really have time to discuss it with anyone.

As she pulled up to the barber shop on 9 Forest Street, she couldn't believe her eyes.

The front of the old house up to the fence was roped off with yellow police tape and there was glass all over the front porch. The chair out front had been over turned and the big bay window with "Jacob's Barber Shop" hand decaled on the glass was now a gaping hole. Lisa pulled over and parked at the sidewalk. The nearest police officer approached her, waving his hand at her.

"I'm sorry, I can't let you go back there ma'am."

"I work here, where's Orv? What happened? Is everything ok?"

"Mr. Byron is over there," he said, pointing at the side of the building. There was Orv, talking to a round bellied detective that was smoking a fat cigar and listening intently to Orv's story. "Detective Sherluck will want to talk to you, too, miss." Lisa stumbled in the direction of his outstretched finger and dazedly shook her head while she surveyed the scene. She didn't interrupt the men as they approached.

"Mr. Byron, I think rock was thrown from inside the shop," the detective told him, generously puffing his cigar. Orv flexed his hands nervously.

"But how is that even possible? Are you saying it's an inside job?" Orv looked even more distressed. The cigar wobbled as the detective spoke.

"That's exactly what it was. Look," he said pointing. "All the glass is on the outside of the shop. Not a piece inside. The door is locked. Someone that had a key threw the brick from the inside after ransacking the place and then walked out the front door and locked it. The perfect crime," he surmised, patting his belly. Lisa stared with her mouth open.

"Do you have a key, miss?" he asked her.

"No, I don't have a key, my co-worker Ashley and the cleaning crew has keys," replied Lisa.

"That cleaning crew! I'll tell them not to come back," he said. Lisa shook her head.

"Don't be hasty, Orv. You don't know anything yet." Orv was convinced otherwise, and waved her off, muttering. She turned her attention back to the detective.

"Was anything stolen?" she asked him.

"Was anything stolen?!" exclaimed Orv. "Hell yes, something was stolen. My whole book of blank checks, and a weeks' worth of revenue! All the deposit slips and all of the cash in lock box is gone." Lisa was shocked and shook her head.

"What can I do?" she asked. She looked towards the door of the shop and saw a lady officer coming out of the crime scene with an evidence kit. The detective tamped the ash on his cigar and pointed.

"We're about cleared out in there," he said to Lisa and Orv. Orv looked back at the shop.

"I'll go in and get started cleaning up, Orv." she said, turning away and trudging up to the porch of the barber shop. The detective nodded and Orv motioned her away, staying.

Lisa peered in the door of the shop and was relieved. There wasn't too much damage, just a few shards of glass that had fallen from the window. The real mess was in Orv's office. The cash box had been taken for evidence but the papers and files were all over the place and his chair was overturned like the one outside. She grabbed the broom and started sweeping up the glass shards. Lisa put right the chair and started picking up Orv's papers. Ashley was due in today, and the mess would be gone before then.

Ashley did come in that afternoon, and was shocked to find out that the barber shop had been robbed. The glass had been repaired and cleaned up, so it wasn't obvious at first. She cut hair as usual and went about her business. Orv stayed all day and locked the shop up himself, counting out the tickets. He wasn't taking any chances, and Lisa noticed that he was keeping a close eye on his hair dressers. Gabriella hadn't shown up, but it was her day off. It went on like that for a week, with Orv coming in and staying all day. It was taking its toll on him, and he was doing fewer haircuts these days, spending more time in his office instead.

There hadn't been any leads on the break in at the shop, but one afternoon the phone rang in the shop and Orv answered it. He listened to the other end of the line and his face looked grim while he pressed the phone up to his ear. He watched Ashley and Lisa cut hair, and then hung up the phone as Gabriella waltzed through the door. Orv wasted no time.

"You're late," Orv said to her, hands on his hips.

"Only a couple of minutes," said Gabriella. "It is three minutes after 1," she told him, checking her watch.

"You're fired." Orv said it bluntly, without preamble. Being late was a pet peeve of his, and he would often cold shoulder the tardy person until he finally gave up being perturbed and warmed back up. He didn't seem like he was in a mood for jovial antics when he approached her, and she left without saying a word. When he told Gabriella she was fired, Ashley stopped cutting hair and turned toward the mirror. Orv walked over to her.

"Ashley, is there something you want to tell me?" His eyes bore directly into hers. She looked away.

"No," she stammered. He glowered at her. Lisa was confused.

"Ashley is there something you'd like to tell me?" he asked her again.

"Well, I..." Ashley trailed off. Orv watched her carefully. He spoke to Lisa.

"That was the detective. He said that he knew who had broken into the shop that evening, and it turns out that it *was* an inside job. Said he tracked down a blank check that had been stolen from here and attempted to be cashed at the Mobil station up the road." He looked at Ashley. Tears slid down her face, and she threw up her hands.

"Are you going to press charges?" She was on the verge of dropping to her knees and begging. He eyed her speculatively.

"I don't know, can you tell the truth?"

"I'm sorry, Mr. Orv, I needed the money, please don't press charges." The words all but exploded out of her. The customer in the chair got up and walked out, haircut unfinished. Orv nodded and waved him out, telling him to come back in later on that afternoon. Ashley sat down in the chair and began her confession.

"I've wanted to leave town for months now, but I haven't had the money. There's a rehab center in Tucson, where my mom is. She told me she'd put me up if I bought my own plane ticket out of here. The cocaine was mine, too." Ashley put her hands over her face and bent over, sobbing openly. Orv looked away and Lisa rolled her eyes. She had seen this coming, somehow. She looked tearfully up at Orv. He shook his head and sighed.

"Ashley, you do good work, but you can't stay here. I'll call the detective back and tell him I won't press charges on you, but you don't work here anymore. You also owe me money which I'll be taking out of your next commission pay. I'll leave you enough money to take the bus." Orv strode into his office and slammed the door behind him. Lisa looked at Ashley, and turned away. Lisa was sorry for her illness and sorry that Ashley had resorted to stealing in order to survive, but she couldn't see a more fitting punishment than getting fired, so said nothing to the woman that she had known. Ashley just gathered up her things, and started to walk out the door. She paused and looked back; Lisa looked up.

"Sorry," she said, fidgeting with the zipper on her sweater. She shrugged and Lisa nodded.

"It's cool," Lisa said lightly. "Good luck, and keep out of trouble. I'm sure there's a salon or two in Tucson." She turned away again, wiping the counters free of dust. Orv didn't come out of his office until it got busy, and even then, didn't have much to say. When he did come out, he walked up to her and handed her an envelope full of money.

21

"This is the pay that you deserved when you told me the first time that they had been messing with the tickets." He passed her a key. "Here's a key to the shop, I can't do this by myself, and I'd like you to stay." She looked at him and nodded.

"What about Ruby?" she asked him. Ruby had been on vacation and would be coming in the next day to help, as it was Friday.

"I don't know, Lisa." Orv shook his head, and wondered what he was going to do. The day passed with the two of them cutting hair and keeping clean. Orv left an hour early and let her close up the shop. He was just too tired. Lisa came in early the next day to help Orv get set up. Ruby came in at one o'clock that afternoon, and it was none too soon – Orv had gone home after he had fixed the books and done a couple of shaves. Lisa had customers lined up and was cutting hair as fast as she could. Ruby came in and washed up immediately.

"Where's Gabbie?" she asked Lisa after a while.

"Gabbie doesn't work here anymore. Orv fired her."

"What? What do you mean 'fired her'?"

"There was a break in last week, and he got fed up with Gabbie's behavior so he fired her on the spot. Ashley got fired, too." Lisa looked sad.

"Why did Ashley get fired?" Ruby looked confused and shocked.

"She staged the break in and then tried to cash a check that she stole from Orv."

"This is ridiculous; Gabbie shouldn't have been fired for that. Ashley broke in, not her."

"Ruby, Gabbie got fired because she's constantly late."

"Well, I still don't think that it's right to punish her because someone else messed up." Lisa wasn't going to argue. As far as she was concerned, Ruby was cut from the same cloth as Gabriella, and Lisa didn't like it. Ruby fell silent until the shop got quiet and got on the phone with Orv. Lisa eavesdropped unabashedly.

"Mr. Orv," said Ruby, "You need to give Gabbie another chance. She didn't do anything wrong. I promise she'll be in on time from now on, and Ashley's not here to influence her, so you

22

should try her again." She listened intently and they spoke for a few more minutes. Ruby hung up.

"So did you get your friend her job back?" Lisa asked Ruby.

"Yes, and she'll be in tomorrow." Ruby looked smug and Lisa was a bit disgusted by the whole thing. As she closed the shop that night, she thought about striking out on her own and dreamed of owning her own shop.

Ruby made good on her promise and for the first few weeks, Gabriella was on time and good for working. Ruby was working on a regular basis, and Orv was more frequently leaving the three of them alone in the shop as he had when it was Ashley and Lisa. And just like before, Gabriella started spending more time in the bathroom and Ruby would often come in hung over. Lisa waited until they were both supposed to be there and called Orv to tell him what was going on. This time, Orv marched up to the shop and changed his mind. He waited in his office until they were both there and then came out. They both looked completely surprised. He addressed them.

"Ruby, you and your girlfriend have to go. We're not doing this. You're late all the time and you come in half drunk. Gabbie, if she shows up, comes in late and makes up her mind that she's going to be here whenever she wants. You can either finish up today or you can go home now." Orv looked at them both sternly. Lisa just calmly massaged the customer's scalp that she had been shampooing. Inside, she was jumping up and down. It would be her and Orv for a while, but that was ok. It was work.

It wasn't long before it wasn't ok. The customers that Ashley and Gabriella had accrued while at the shop still wanted to come and see Lisa – even though they weren't her clients. Orv was working overtime and although Lisa was opening and closing the shop every night for Orv, he was there a lot. Orv was tired – or his health was failing him. He spent more and more time in his office, and he did fewer and fewer haircuts. It wasn't until his twin walked in that Orv finally saw some relief on the horizon.

Damien wasn't really Orv's twin, in fact, he was absolutely no relation, but he could have been Orv's son. He was tall and thin like Orv, and even wore the same spectacles. He had come in the shop one Friday afternoon and told Orv that he needed a job.

"Well, can you cut hair?" Orv asked Damien. "How long have you been doing it?"

"I've been cutting hair for about a year. I quit my job as a used car salesman and started cutting hair. I've got some pretty unique styles, and I am the Big Kahuna of the Chair." Orv chuckled and nodded at him. Lisa was confused.

"The Big Kahuna of the Chair?"

"You know," said Damien, "the big cheese. I'm the king of haircuts, the Big Kahuna of the chair." Orv sniffed and pursed his lips together as if biting off a retort. He was slow to reply.

"Well, I guess you can't do any more harm than has been done. Come back Monday at 1 o'clock." Damien shook his hand pleasantly and walked out of the shop. At least that was solved.

Damien did come back on Monday, but Lisa wondered if he was even the same man that she had met that Friday. He seemed moody and he wasn't getting along very well with Orv. Orv came in one morning and Damien was arguing with Jerry about whether or not he wanted a haircut.

"I don't want no haircut, I want a shave! Where's Orv?" he asked Damien.

"The old man isn't here you'll just have to do without him today." Damien got the straight razor and smoothed it across a leather strap that hung along the counter bar.

"You aren't touching me with no straight razor! I'll wait for Lisa." Lisa was washing a client's hair in preparation for a cut, who wouldn't mind waiting with Jerry while they sat together. Lisa would pile Jerry's face up with towels and they would sit and chat. Then she would cut hair.

"What does she know? Does she shave her face?" Damien retorted. He hadn't seen Orv walk in. Lisa snorted and raised her eyebrows at Orv behind Damien's back.

"She knows a heck of a lot more than you do," he said to Damien. Damien whirled around and glared at him with furious guilt and Orv ignored it. Lisa thought Damien was rude and Damien did he best to fit the bill. He would often glare at her while she was cutting hair and one day he claimed that he was copying his style. She had given a lady a haircut called The Rachel, a layered bob that was popular on television at the time, and Damien huffed and puffed until the customer left. When she did, Damien started in on Lisa.

"What is it that you think you're doing copying my style?" he asked her bluntly, pushing his glasses up on his nose.

"Excuse me?" asked Lisa. "That's a really common haircut and I learned it in hairdressing school."

"Oh bull, you copied me and you know it. I've been doing that haircut for years!" he exclaimed.

"I thought you said that you'd only been hairdressing for a year," Lisa retorted, getting angry at his tone and accusations.

"I thought it up years ago, but I didn't call it whatever stupid name you just said."

"So did you think up the TV show that made it popular too? And I suppose you dreamed up how to put a bowl over someone's head and cut the bottom off" Lisa could feel the top of her head overheating. "Because that's about what all of your haircuts look like."

Damien looked as if he had slapped her, and was deeply insulted. His ideas were fresh and innovative, and she and the old man were clearly copying his superior style. That's alright. He knew that he was a better barber than the two of them put together anyhow. He would show them both. He knew what he was doing and he wasn't going let anyone steal from him. His attitude toward Lisa for the rest of the day was dour and mean, but he didn't say much.

The next day, Orv didn't come in at all. He had woken that morning and his left foot was swollen so he went to the doctor instead of coming in. Damien talked trash about Orv the entire day, until Lisa was fed up with it. She remained silent and was immensely relieved when his shift ended and she turned off the pole as she locked the door behind him. She swept the floor and wiped down all the chairs for the final time, leaving the trash in the buckets for the cleaning crew – which Orv had rehired – to pick up when they came in later that evening. Lisa picked up a small scrap of paper that had drifted to the side and she saw that it was a crumpled up ticket for a straight razor shave dated for that day. There was only one customer that got only a shave – and he had been here today. Damien must have forgotten to put it on the peg. She carried it over to register where she began to tally the prices on the ticket.

She added the figures up once, and then a second time to be sure, but by the third time she added up all of the tickets – including Damien's lost ticket – Lisa was positive that the money in the register was exactly twelve dollars short – the price of the "daily shave." When she took out Damien's ticket, the numbers added up exactly. Lisa rolled her eyes and shook her head, feeling awful for Orv. She put the missing ticket with the others and pulled twelve dollars out of her own purse, putting it with the rest of the money from the till. Orv didn't need any more drama, and Lisa didn't have the energy to fight with him.

It was a good thing too, because Orv called Lisa that night and asked her to open the shop for him. It wasn't unusual for her to open the shop, but tomorrow was Tuesday, a day that he reserved for his regulars' haircuts and opened the barber shop himself. He told her that he had gone to the doctor that morning about his feet, and the doctor had run some tests on him. He had diabetes and was already suffering from heart disease. He had advised Al to take a month off from standing on his feet and let someone else run the shop. Lisa spoke up right away.

"If you'll make Damien's schedule, I can come in and open and then stay until closing. I don't have anything pressing right now, so it's no big deal."

"You sure do know how to run my shop, don't you?" He was trying to joke with her, but she could hear the note of rancor in his statement.

"No, that's not it, Mr. Orv, come on. You know I care about you; I'm just trying to help. Besides, if I want to run the shop I'll just partner up with you!" Lisa was trying to be lighthearted back, but she had failed miserably as well. She had been considering asking him to partner with her, but she hadn't approached him.

"Come on, if you want to run a shop, you can get your own."

"I just might do that!" Lisa had been thinking about it for quite

26

some time now.

"Cut your nose off to spite your face? It'll be the death of your career! You leave and your so called salon will be so dusty that you won't be able to turn the pole on without an apron! Would you like to beg for your job now or later?" Lisa rolled her eyes on the other end of the line. This was Orv being funny.

She laughed off the comments and hung up with him, turning over and thinking for a long time what it would be like to own her own hair salon. Lisa knew what Orv said wasn't exactly true. She had a few regulars that came to her, and had even gained the trust of old timers like Jerry and a few others that claimed she was the first woman to ever cut their hair. She never knew when she fell asleep.

The next six weeks at Jacob's Barbershop were a living hell. Orv had waited until both she and Damien were there and called them both in his office while there were no customers.

"Alright, I've decided to stay out for six weeks instead of just a month." Before he could go further, Damien started.

"What's the matter, can't hack it?" Damien chuckled meanly. Orv ignored him and addressed Lisa, which made Damien blush and fold his arms. He didn't say anything else for a moment.

"Lisa, I'm leaving you in charge of the shop. You have a key; I'll leave you one for the deposit box and my office. The ticket system and the register procedures stay the same. You're to leave the money in the deposit box overnight and then in the morning when the bank opens or you go on lunch, then you can take it to the bank. Damien, I've got you scheduled for the busiest part of the day, and you're to come in at 10am and stay till 6pm Monday through Friday. That should be sufficient to help Lisa, shouldn't it?" He still wasn't looking at Damien. Lisa nodded.

"I'll be back on Thursday to do the payroll," he said, handing her a set of keys. "Take care of the shop," he said to her. Lisa nodded, feeling sad. The rest of day remained uneventful, except for Damien.

"He'll be back on Thursday to do the payroll? What payroll, he doesn't pay enough! That's alright though, I get mine. I'll get mine. You should get yours too," He nodded his head as if that was

27

that. Lisa thought she was confused, but it wasn't until that night when she added up the money that she knew something was off again, and remembered the ticket from the other night. She didn't have the heart to bother Orv with it.

Damien complained more and more each day as the weeks passed, and was openly pocketing money. What was more? He was doing his best to ruin Orv altogether. He would tell Orv's customers that they looked better than ever, and invited them to call upon him any time they needed a haircut – especially after Orv came back. Orv had been gone for three weeks and one day, Damien was complaining heavily about Orv's payroll to Lisa.

"He doesn't pay me enough, and he's taxing us to death." he complained, as he crumpled up the ticket that Lisa had called him out on. "I told you, I was going to get mine. You should get yours too. I already called the labor board on him. Just ring one ticket and then keep one." She wasn't comfortable with lying and stealing, so she just continued to do what Orv had asked her to do without comment. It wasn't until the IRS called the shop looking for Orv that she decided to blow the whistle. She called him from the salon to speak with him.

"Damien has been taking money out of the till and isn't ringing his tickets. And he called the IRS and tried to say that you weren't handling your taxes properly." Orv huffed on the end of the line, but didn't say much.

"I'll be back in a couple of weeks," he said. "Just keep your peepers open until then." Lisa did, and then Orv was subpoenaed. He came to the shop with his papers and holed up in his office until it was time to close the shop. He came out with a sheaf of papers. Lisa was ringing out the tickets.

"What's happening, Orv?"

"He wasn't kidding. Damien called the board of labor and the damned IRS telling them that I don't take care of my books, and I don't pay him all of his hours that he works."

"He's been skipping haircuts too. He pockets every other haircut without writing a ticket for it. I've watched him do it and he wanted me to do the same." Lisa was blunt about all that she had seen, just as she had with been with him at the time with

Ashley and Gabriella. She was furious – *why* wouldn't he do anything? '*Because you couldn't force the truth out of people,*' he would always say, '*but the truth will usually force itself out.*' Orv shook his head.

"I know you wouldn't do that, Lisa." Orv knew her by now, but what else could he do? For years, he had been Orv Byron, New Canaan's oldest and best barber and he had spent his whole life waking up every day and turning on the pole. Lisa had worked with him for almost two years now. Orv shuffled around and ran his hand along the handle of the door. Lisa felt sorry for him.

"I'll still help you run the shop, Orv." He turned to her.

"I'm going to fire him when this is over," he said to her. Lisa nodded.

CHAPTER 4:
A NEW BEGINNING

Lisa had worked with Orv for well over two years now. She had been by his side, and sat with him during the roughest times in his career – which was saying a lot because he had been a barber for a very long time. She had tried one more time to get Orv to  partner with her, and the conversation had ended in an argument that had almost gotten her fired. He would be Orv Byron the Barber, forever, and it would never be "Orv and Lisa, the best barber/styling team on the whole planet." As she sat outside the bank with her brief case in her hand, she cried. Lisa had been turned down for another loan yet again.

They were tears of anger. It wasn't as though she had terrible credit – she just didn't have any at all. She was young, and banks just weren't in the business of loaning money to people that didn't have any credit. Lisa had several credit cards with decent limits and she knew what had to be done. She knew, she just knew! Lisa had built up a nice list of clientele that she was sure would follow her if she opened a new salon. She maxed out her credit cards and put a deposit down in the upstairs part of a building on Locust Street in New Canaan. It would be called Lisa's Classic Cuts and she would run it herself. Damn Orv, and what he said about her career. She could do it.

And she did. The upstairs shop was nice, and Lisa made flyers and signs for people to follow up the stairs. She was building up a decent business, and most of her clients had followed her. She was getting overwhelmed and it seemed that Someone was listening, because on a day that she lifted her eyes to the sky and said, "I need help," the phone rang out of the blue. It was Gabriella, the hairdresser that Orv had fired for being late.

"Lisa, I heard that you've opened up a shop and I need a good job." Gabriella said to her over the phone. Gabriella had bad habits and her instincts were screaming at her to remember it, but Lisa needed help. Gabriella also had a knack for coloring and cutting hair.

"Are you cleaned up? Because if you pull the same crap on me that you pulled at Jacob's Barber Shop, I'll have you arrested in a heartbeat and sent to jail for as long as they'll hold you." It wasn't a threat. Lisa was serious. Gabriella huffed a little sigh on other end of the line – not a mean one, but a weary one.

"Yes, I've cleaned up. I don't even mess with the same crowd. I just want honest work." Lisa couldn't find a reason to argue with that, and besides she needed help that knew how to cut hair.

"Alright then, I need someone to do colors and perms and highlights. You in?"

"Definitely, when can I come in?" At least she was eager, thought Lisa.

"You can come in tomorrow if you like. We'll set you up a chair."

"Great," exclaimed Gabriella. "I'll be there." Lisa hung up with her and went about her day. Things were looking up.

Gabriella came in on time, and dressed professionally, ready to work. She did well, and she and Lisa worked well together. She was never late and never complained. It really seemed that she had turned her life around. Lisa cut hair and Gabriella performed highlights, and it got to where business was so good that she had to hire someone else. Lisa put an ad in the paper and a beautiful young Honduran woman named Angelica. Angelica's mother was a hair dresser in Honduras and she knew what she was doing. When she told Lisa that she often cut her own hair, Lisa was impressed. She had a fantastic style. Angelica wasn't much older than 19.

Angelica and Gabriella worked well together too, and Lisa felt comfortable leaving the shop. She would open the shop, and then Gabriella and Angelica would cut hair alone in the afternoons. It was a good deal, until Lisa noticed that there was less and less money being made on days they were left alone together. She inwardly groaned and remembered all the times she had wanted to put herself in Orv's shoes. She waited until Gabriella was gone one afternoon and approached Angelica, who was sweeping the floor.

"Angelica, how many haircuts did you do yesterday?" Lisa started. Angelica looked nervous.

"Twelve, why?" asked Angelica, turning away. Lisa watched her and her instincts told her to poke some more.

"How many colors did Gabbie do yesterday?" Angelica had picked up a dust rag and started wiping down her chair and her hand froze when Lisa asked about Gabriella. Lisa thought her stomach was going to drop out and Angelica would swear later that she felt electricity in the air between them as a short silence crackled between them. She looked at the chair and moved her hand once in a circle nervously. Lisa watched her and she saw the woman cut her eyes to the side and nod her head decisively once before looking directly at her and answering.

"She did eight highlights yesterday, and made an appointment for a private perm." Angelica had tears in her eyes that spilled down her olive cheeks, but she looked Lisa in the eye. She was telling the truth, but not all of Gabriella's slips had been put into the till. There were only three color slips and there certainly wasn't anything on the appointment books about a perm. Angelica finished wiping the chair vigorously and she spoke to Lisa, not looking at her.

"Lisa we were very poor until my mother started cutting hair in Honduras. I was about five, I guess. Some of the other poor kids in Santa Rita would steal their food while others would stand in the street and beg for work. My mother would not allow us to steal and every night she reminded us that God would provide if we kept His word. She worked and she taught me how to work. That woman that works here, she doesn't belong here. She steals your money." Lisa liked Angelica more than ever, and she thanked her, vowing to confront Gabriella in the morning when she came in.

Lisa was in the shop an hour before it was due to open. She had a moment of nostalgia when she unlocked the door, and almost yearned for the red and white pole at Jacob's. Gabriella waltzed in with a bright smile, and greeted her. Lisa wanted to kick her ass, but she was better than that so she just smiled back and crooked her finger at Gabriella.

"Come on back here for a second, Gabbie." Lisa went into the storeroom that she kept a tiny desk and a data computer on with a printer, as well as all of the supplies that overflowed from the tiny room she used as a stock room. A folding chair served as a "guest seat." Gabriella sat down in it. Lisa didn't waste time.

"I know you've been doing more jobs than you put slips in for."

"What?"

Lisa snorted. *"I know you've been doing more jobs than you put slips in for."* She repeated it slowly as if she was talking to a child. Gabriella was trying to look bewildered and not doing a good job. Lisa just watched her fidget.

"What makes you say that? If this is about that Angelica girl maybe you should ask her about how many jobs I do." Lisa laughed out loud. She already had asked Angelica. She had also taken the time to count the supplies and add the differences up to make sure that Angelica didn't have anything to hide. The numbers told the truth. The fact that Gabriella was dropping names amused her. She sobered and eyed Gabriella with a level stare.

"Look Gabbie, you have a choice. You can either tell the truth or I can call the police and tell him to come pick you up right now. You've either been stealing my money, or you've been taking highlight kits home because there are only three slips and there's five more kits missing. So, which is it?"

Gabriella's eyes filled with tears.

"Don't call the cops," she croaked at Lisa.

"Then tell me the deal, or I'll press charges." Lisa was firm but Gabriella was dissolving into tears.

"I needed the money." Gabriella said lamely. She sounded so much like Ashley right then that Lisa knew she had been lied to. Gabriella wasn't clean at all.

"For drugs?" Lisa asked. Gabriella nodded.

"Damn it Gabbie, you told me you were cleaned up. I took a chance on you."

"I'm sorry, Lisa, please." Lisa pointed at the door.

"You have to go," Lisa said stoutly. "I won't call the cops; I'm not going there with you, but you're out. Clean out your station and leave. Don't put my name on your resume, that's a bad move." Gabriella gathered up her stuff and left Lisa's office without saying a word. Lisa got up and shut the door behind her for a brief moment. Her head was swimming and she needed to catch her breath. Is this how Orv felt? The bell that she had hung on the door tinkled and she went out to the waiting room to see her first customer. It was still very early.

It was a new customer that Lisa hadn't seen before and she looked like she was scoping the place out. Lisa liked her immediately. The woman had striking blonde hair and looked to be about the same age. Lisa could tell that her blonde was out of the bottle, although her roots were well tended. She was finely dressed and wearing a wedding ring. Lisa smiled at her.

"Hi, I'm Lisa, welcome!" she said with a heartiness she didn't feel. The woman gave her a tentative smile back. She stood in the middle of the shop, and that was when Lisa noticed the car seat at her feet, rocking gently with a tap of Anne's toes.

"Hi, Lisa, I'm Anne. I saw one of your signs and thought I would give you a try." Anne patted her hair. "I'm in the market for a hairdresser that knows what's up." Lisa nodded firmly.

"I got this!" Lisa said to her. She gestured for Anne to have a seat. Lisa went over and grabbed the car seat, putting the infant right next to one of the barber chairs. She patted the leather chair invitingly and Anne gave a little sigh of something like relief. Anne sat up in the salon chair and helped the hairdresser adjust the smock she had draped over Anne. Lisa leaned her back and started to give her a wash. She struck up a conversation with Lisa while the hot water felt so heavenly..

"So have you been here long?" Anne asked her.

"Well, I used to cut hair for Jacob's Barber Shop but I wanted my own space, ya know? Something that was mine."

"I definitely know how you feel." Anne was new in town and looking for a niche of her own to fall into. Lisa picked up on this right away.

"This is a pretty small town and I haven't seen you around.

Are you visiting for the summer?"

"No, I just moved here with my husband and four children."

"Oh, you have other kids? How old?" Anne felt a knot of dread work into her stomach.

"Well, Ieva is almost eight, and Robbie just turned six. Karl is four and this is Erik. He's the littlest of the bunch, obviously." She didn't elaborate further. Lisa thought she just might be nervous about meeting someone new, so she did her best to break the ice.

"Wow, I bet they love school! Will Ieva be going into the third grade this year?"

"Yea, Ieva and Robbie like school very much, and Karl is going to be in pre-school this year." She didn't mention their grades.

"Well that's nice, New Canaan has a really great elementary school, and the upper level teachers are really good. They take the older grades on some interesting field trips every year, and during the season, they bring all the kids to the Nature Center in New Canaan and let them explore." She dumped some shampoo into her palm and massaged Anne's scalp. Anne was silent. "What grade will Ieva be in this year?" She wasn't sure but thought she had already asked. Anne closed her eyes and took a deep breath. Here it comes, she thought.

"First," she said slowly. Lisa stopped massaging for a split second and added up what Anne had told her in her head. Ieva was eight; she should be in third grade. Obviously, that wasn't so. The baby started to snuffle in his car seat but other than that, the room was silent except for the air conditioning. Lisa didn't want to drive Anne away, and was afraid to even ask. Anne however was used to a lot more than polite questioning from a hair dresser, so she answered Lisa's unspoken question.

"Ieva has Down syndrome," Anne said bluntly. "She's in the same grade with Robbie." Lisa sighed with relief.

"Oh is that all?! I thought you were going to tell me something terrible like she hated school and locked herself in the basement when you tried to take her," Lisa exclaimed. Anne laughed out loud in her shock. She had heard some hurtful things in her day about little Ieva, and was relieved that Lisa had tried to lighten the

35

situation. Sure, it was a terrible joke, but at least it hadn't been a mean comment – and Anne was deeply appreciative. Sometimes, a little acceptance was all that was needed, and it seemed that Lisa didn't care one whit. She liked Lisa. Lisa liked her too. Anne wasn't going to tell her that she had come here to test the waters to see if Ieva would be welcome here in the shop. She obviously would be.

Lisa asked Anne what kind of haircut she wanted and Anne took a shot in the dark. She shrugged.

"I don't know, do something nice," she challenged Lisa. Lisa flipped through a magazine or two, periodically looking at Anne, and occasionally turning her head this way or that. She closed the magazines and nodded firmly, turning Anne away from the mirror so that she couldn't see. They chatted and became fast friends in the shop that day, while the salon continued to fill up with people. When Lisa finally turned Anne around, she was mesmerized at her own reflection. Lisa had done something wonderful with her hair. Anne would be coming back soon with her children, and would definitely be coming back for her own haircuts. She left Lisa's shop with a smile, and everywhere she went, people complimented her style. Lisa had definitely proved she was something special.

She was blessed when none other than Orv called to tell her that the lease on a ground level building that had been a salon became available to her in her price range and spent the next 47 nights in a row closing the upstairs salon and moving it piece by piece.

CHAPTER 5:
RETURN OF THE BIG KAHUNA

The move turned out to be a boon. By the time Lisa had fired Gabriella and had met Anne, she was still getting swamped with clients both new and old. It was just her and Angelica running the shop – Angelica was still a phenomenal hairdresser and she was still as honest and hardworking as the day she had walked in. She had even helped with the move. Still, it was becoming too much for the two of them.

Angelica's mother was opening up another salon in her home country, and Angelica had expressed that she would like to go and help. Lisa had to fight the urge to drop to her knees each and every time they discussed it and beg Angelica not to go. Instead, she simply put an ad in the classifieds and took interviews. There was only one good prospect so far but she needed one more to help carry the load when Angelica left. As she sat at her office desk early one morning and chewed on the end of her pencil, she took the plunge and picked up the phone book. Sliding her finger down the page and finding the number, Lisa took the phone off the hook and dialed it.

"Hello?" was the answer from the other end of the line.

"Damien?"

"Yes, who is this?"

"Damien, this is Lisa, from Jacob's Barber Shop." Lisa thought for a moment that she must be out of her mind. It was confirmed when Damien answered.

"Oh yes, that little girlie that stole my styles. No matter. What can I do for ya, gal?" Lisa gritted her teeth and bit the bullet.

"I started my own shop. I need a good barber. Would you like to work?"

"Well sure, I could use the money!" Damien sounded elated. "What made you call me?"

I had a few drinks before I went to work today, she thought, and laughed out loud at the smart, unspoken retort before answering. She put on her best kissing voice and laid it on for him.

"Well what salon would be complete without the Big Kahuna of Haircuts?" Damien laughed out loud with her.

"I guess you're right. Sure, I'll work for you." She thanked him and told him to come in Monday, hanging up the phone. Lisa pinched the bridge of her nose and put her head down on the desk. When the bell tinkled as it had when she had met Anne, she went out to see who was in the shop. It was her interviewee. He was tall and lithe, and his shirt spoke louder than he did, but he still was immaculately dressed.

"Hi! I'm Percy!" he said to her, and thrust his hand out so she could shake it. He spoke with a lisp, and walked with a little frisk in his hips. Lisa had a deep suspicion that he was...*well never mind.* She smiled.

"Hi, Percy, I'm Lisa." She shook his hand and it was firm. "How long have you been a hairdresser?"

"I've been a hairdresser since I was four, and licensed for about ten years now. I would steal my sister's dolls and give them new haircuts. She loved it." He looked around. "I just love this place," he said to her. "All this is yours?"

Lisa swelled with pride.

"Yes it is! I've been here for about nine months. Not a bad deal. I need another barber, though."

Percy snapped his fingers and shook his finger at her.

"No honey, I'm a hairdresser. I make people look good, not just cut hair." Lisa couldn't help but laugh. He was everything she needed.

"Well, I could use one of those too. Are you available Monday? I'd like you to start."

"Sure. I have one slight issue though." Lisa sank.

"What's that?"

"I'm gay." Percy stepped back and looked at her for her

reaction. Those "drinks" must have gone to Lisa's head after she called Damien this morning, because she blurted out, "Well, duh." Percy just laughed at her.

"No! I mean, well...you know what I mean. Is it ok if sometimes Nigel brings me flowers and stuff at work, or brings me my lunch?"

"Oh, well that's fine," she said, relieved. "I just don't want to find you in the stockroom with him or anything."

"Oh you won't, Miss Lisa."

"Good, come in Monday. Everyone will be here then." Lisa dismissed him, and he left, swishing his hips back and forth as he walked out the door. He did a little dance in front of the window that she was sure she wasn't supposed to see. Angelica came in later that afternoon and laughed at the description of Percy and again at the idea of the Big Kahuna of Haircuts. The rest of week passed without event.

Damien and Percy arrived at the same time on Monday morning. Percy looked immaculate in slacks and a dress shirt, and Damien had chosen his old hair cutting smock. They both looked like heaven to Lisa, who already had a salon full of people. She put them each at a station let them do their thing. Percy had a way with the customers and people loved him immediately. He was kind to them and didn't make a fuss when they complimented his work. He just thanked them and sent them out. Damien was himself in a good mood, and stayed that way until Nigel walked in on Percy's lunch hour. He had brought Percy a box lunch and a bouquet of flowers. Damien eyed them suspiciously and his mouth dropped open when they gently kissed on the lips and hugged at the end of the meeting. Damien found Lisa in the back room and tapped her on the shoulder.

"Did you know you hired a gay?" he asked without preamble.

"Man, what?" Lisa asked, annoyed at the interruption.

"Did. You. Know. You. Hired. A. Gay." He said it as if she were a child.

"A gay?"

"Percy."

"I knew Percy was a homosexual, yes. Is there a problem with that?" Lisa wasn't looking for a reason to fire Damien, but if she did, she was guessing that this would be it. There wasn't a lot Lisa couldn't stomach, but intolerance was one of them. Damien sniffed and shook his head.

"I guess not." He turned away and went back to work and Lisa sighed with relief. That was one thing she didn't want to deal with. Damien did a good job of hiding his feelings for about a week. He asked to change stations with Lisa, saying that he preferred to be closer to the stock room, so Lisa switched. She knew he was trying to get away from Percy, but didn't say a word. Percy cornered her in the stock room one afternoon.

"Ooh, Miss Lisa! He does *not* like me. I know he switched with you to put you between us." He grabbed the box that she was emptying onto the shelves and helped her put the stuff away.

"Has he said anything to you out of the way?" The last thing she wanted was a war in her salon.

"No," sighed Percy, "But he doesn't have to. I've met his kind of man before. He's so scared I'm going to hit on him that he'd burst into flames if I said hello to him." Lisa laughed despite herself.

"He got mad at me the other day too, it was really weird." Lisa stopped stocking.

"What happened?"

"He said that I looked at him while he was giving a haircut and then tried to cop his style. He also accused me of taking pictures of his haircuts with my camera. Lisa, I don't even have a camera, he's lost." Lisa knew what Percy was talking about; she had experienced it for herself. It was par for the course. If someone so much as glanced at Damien while he was giving a haircut, he would get moody and weird for the rest of the day, and snap impatiently at everyone. When Lisa and Damien had worked for Orv, it was days like these that ended in a pregnant silence.

"Well, I apologize on his behalf." Lisa took the empty box from him.

"Don't worry honey, I don't know how long I can take his crap, but I like you!" With that, he popped a kiss on her cheek and flounced away. Damien on the other hand wasn't so accepting. All hell broke loose one afternoon a while later when he lost his glasses and gave three bad haircuts in a row. Lisa had already heard them arguing out front about whether or not "Percy was looking at Damien." Damien hadn't changed in the slightest bit, but this wasn't that kind of argument. Lisa could hear Percy yelling at Damien.

"Oh my god, you let that lady walk out of here looking like that?" she heard Percy exclaim. Damien slammed a pair of scissors on the counter.

"She looks better than you do,"

"Oh *honey*, no woman looks better than me, and don't forget it." Percy snapped his fingers and walked back to Lisa's office. He stopped at the door and put his hands on his hips. He looked up at her.

"Mom, Grandpa lost his glasses and he's been forgetting to hand out paper bags with his haircuts, I think you need to talk to him," Percy said nastily, and turned and walked out. Lisa banged her head on the desk before walking out.

"What's wrong?!" she snapped at the pair of them. "Damien, did you lose your glasses?"

"Yes, I lost my glasses, but Liberace here is no help."

"He's going to ruin you, Miss Lisa. He left a hole in this woman's haircut and had to patch it up by practically scalping her. She looked terrible." Percy held his palm out and studied his fingernails. Damien had his turn.

"He's been taking my styles, too, just like you and that second rate barber up town! I gave a custom haircut yesterday and he turned around and gave the same one to a different gentleman just today."

"If you knew anything about style, you'd know that it's a haircut that's popular. Of course, I can see where you wouldn't. I wouldn't steal something that looked like what you gave that woman today, so you can just keep that one."

"Now see here!" said Damien. Lisa held up her hand. She felt like she was going to blow.

"Stop. Damien, find your glasses. Percy, stop... being honest." Percy snorted and Damien's mouth dropped open. "Damien, I'll

41

clean out the store room and shove everything in my office and you can drag your salon station in there. I'm tired of hearing about how we're stealing your haircuts. We all have the same license. If I get glared at one more time, or another haircut walks out of here that I have to give away or get a complaint about, you're fired. Percy, go home for today. Damien, get in the stock room and start pulling out those boxes along the back wall." She pivoted on her heel and walked back into her office.

Percy stared after her and Damien threw the towel down onto the chair and went into the stock room. Percy tapped on the door of the office.

"You ok?" he asked her. Lisa nodded.

"Yes, I guess I'm ok."

"Sorry about all the noise, I mean…I wish you'd have seen that haircut."

"Did she pay for it?"

"She was too nice to complain," he told her. Lisa shook her head.

"You still want me to go home?" he asked her.

"Yea, go ahead for today. It shouldn't be that busy in here, and I'm going to switch it out so that he can have his little privacy." Percy put his arm around her shoulders.

"You mad at me?" he asked her. Lisa shrugged. Gabriella and Ashley had taken the mickey right out of her for being mad at petty salon drama. There were more things to think about sometimes.

"Nah. All in a day's work." She replied to him. He gave her a little shake and went back to his station, cleaning up his work area and sweeping the floor before he left. She promised to herself that she would make an effort to schedule them separately, at least until Angelica left. She had two weeks to get it together.

Lisa took the rest of the afternoon, and moved Damien into the stockroom. She put all of her stock in the office and lugged Damien's salon chair into the other room. He would have to put his customers in another chair to wash, but when he started cutting, he could come back to the stock room and close the door. There, Damien peacefully co-existed with everyone for months. Percy continued to do fabulous work, Angelica left to help her mother, and Lisa's business was doing better than ever.

One afternoon, all was well in the shop. Lisa was washing a customer's hair, and Percy was coming in from his lunch break. Damien was in the stockroom cutting hair. Percy sat his things down at his station and went to the rest room, which was the door next to the stockroom. It was cracked. Percy and Lisa were chatting, so the man had paused in front of the bathroom door. Damien came to the door and thus began the war.

"What is it exactly that you're doing?" snapped Damien to Percy.

"I'm using the bathroom."

"It looks like you're staring into my booth! Spying on me," he said to Percy.

"I wasn't even looking at you," said Percy rolling his eyes. "I don't see why you're so paranoid, your style is basic stuff that we all learned in school so who is going to steal something they teach for free?" Lisa thought Damien was going to turn purple. Percy went into the restroom and closed the door behind him. Damien approached Lisa.

"If you don't fire that gay, I'm out of here." Lisa hoped *she* wasn't turning purple.

"You know, Damien, I've made enough exceptions for you, and I'm not going to fire him because he's gay, nor am I going to fire him because you don't like him. If you don't like it, there's the door. I *will* fire you for starting an argument with me." Damien wasn't giving up.

"You know, you're just like that Orv, always wanting your employees to go the extra mile for you but never the other way around. He's disgusting trash and he doesn't need to be here."

"Well, I'm sick of your attitude, and I'm not going to fire him. I need him as badly as I need you." Lisa put emphasis on that to remind Damien and herself that she had called Damien and that he needed the job.

"He's bad for business." Lisa scoffed at Damien, but said nothing.

"He's a terrible barber." He tried again.

"He's not a barber, he's a hairdresser," said Lisa.

43

"He's a gay."

Percy exited the bathroom about that time. He walked right up to Damien and waggled a finger in his face, tsking.

"Now, now, if she doesn't fire you I can sue you both Pops for a hostile work environment, but I'd never do that to an employer that treats me well. And yea, I get a lot of crap for being gay, but the difference between me and a lot of people is that I don't care what they think. I don't care what *you* think, Grandpa, but I won't work in a hostile environment with people that think they're better than everyone else." Lisa felt her stomach tighten up. She knew what was coming. "Here in Connecticut we have laws that prohibits discrimination in public and private employment based on gender identity and expression. You can't discharge someone or discriminate against them due to the individual's sexual orientation."

"Percy, no," she begged. *Don't do it man,* she thought furiously.

"I'm sorry Miss Lisa." He said to her. "But you know me better than that. You, on the other hand," he said, pointing his finger at Damien, "wouldn't know your ass from a hole in the ground if it were clearly marked." Damien opened his mouth and closed it back again, looking much like a big fish. Percy gathered up his things, and left them both standing there in the shop. He wouldn't be back, Lisa already knew.

She waggled a finger at Damien.

"If you want to stay here, crawl back in the stockroom, find your glasses, and get to work. I'm really getting tired of your crap."

It was time to place another ad in the paper.

CHAPTER 6:
LISA'S CLASSIC STUNTS

Lisa's ad in the paper hung around for about a week until a short, robust looking woman with long, teased hair walked into the salon. She was an olive tan and had long, false fingernails and dark, lipstick that had begun to dry. She was wearing a low cut shirt and her Capri pants were just a bit tight around the waist line.

"This is your shop?" she asked Lisa, who happened to be washing the front window. Lisa smiled at her, and the woman did not smile back.

"Yes, I own this salon." Lisa replied.

"How old are you?" said the woman. She had a thick accent and Lisa could tell that she was from overseas.

"25," said Lisa. The woman looked astonished and did not bother to conceal her arrogance. Her painted eyebrows crawled comically up her forehead and Lisa wanted to laugh. She didn't get a chance.

"You are too young to have a salon by yourself. You need Raheleh to come and cut hair for you." She shook her finger in Lisa's face. "I do good work," she said.

"You're Raheleh?" Lisa asked.

"Of course I am Raheleh. You put an ad in the paper, yes?"

"Yes."

"I do good work. I cut hair good for you, you hire me."

"No, I think I already have someone chosen from my list of interviewees, thank you."

"You hire me, I work for you. You are too young, you need help." Raheleh insisted. This woman was setting off all kinds of alarm bells in Lisa's head, but she turned them off and insisted her brain go back to sleep. Percy had left, Angelica was gone, and Damien was...well he was Damien and there wasn't anything

45

anyone could do about that. She needed a hair stylist and Raheleh had responded. Raheleh patted her hair.

"I bring you good business. I cut good hair for you." Raheleh was insisting on being a part of her crew and despite her instincts, Lisa told her to come in on Wednesday. Raheleh left the shop, muttering that she would do "good business." Lisa only hoped that she was right. She wasn't the only one that responded to the ad, however, and Lisa was relieved when the two new prospects came in later that week. She still had Damien too, but his attitude with her was getting worse, and he didn't realize that he was standing on his last leg.

Allison had responded to the ad as well, and she was in her mid-thirties. She had children but she was divorced, and was working on her second husband. Moreover, Lisa was delighted to see that she had fabulous hair. Lisa hired her.

Things went well for a few months. Kristie was an excellent hair stylist, and Raheleh was an ok employee. Damien was…well, he was Damien. He stayed in his back room and cut hair, and no one bothered him until he came out. When he did, Raheleh was onto him. Damien would sweep the floor, and Raheleh would complain.

"Didn't your mother teach you good to sweep?" she would ask him.

"What are you even saying to me?" Damien would ask nastily.

"Look at what you missed," she said to him, pointing out tufts of hair and bits of paper that were on the floor.

"You don't need to tell me how to sweep," he snapped at her.

"Well someone should," Raheleh insisted. Damien went back into his stockroom with the broom and didn't come back out that day.

Raheleh and Allison worked well together, although Allison had a few small complaints about Raheleh's behavior.

"Lisa," she said one afternoon, cornering her in the office, "I think you're going to have some problems with Raheleh." Dramatic soap opera violins cued up in her head. She almost giggled.

"What do you mean?" asked Lisa. "Is she getting

46

complaints?"

"Not exactly…" Lisa sighed at Allison.

"Then what?" she asked.

"Well, she's a bit pushy with the customers." Allison looked nervous, as though she were ratting someone out to the principal.

"Pushy?"

"Pushy. She'll stand outside and when someone walks by, she'll drag them inside and tell them that their hair looks awful and that they need a haircut." Lisa's eyes widened. Was Allison serious? Apparently she was, because she continued.

"When it's a woman, she'll drag them inside, but when they are men…when it's a man, she'll rub their shoulders and their arms and tell them how handsome they are, and butter them up. I saw her adjust her clothes to show more." She motioned to her chest.

"Ok, I can talk to her about that."

"Well….there's more." Allison took a deep breath.

"Oh?"

"Yea. Sometimes, when she cuts children's hair, she forces their heads down and pushes them to the side, and when the parents complain, she snaps at them too. I had a lady walk out this past week because Raheleh was cutting another child's hair and was being mean." Allison finally had Lisa's full attention.

"Ok, I'll talk to her." Lisa promised herself that she would talk to Raheleh. Later that afternoon, Lisa's friend Anne came in for a haircut, alone.

"Where's my sweet sugar baby?" Lisa asked her, referring to Erik.

"Ah! I got to leave them all at home with a sitter!" Anne exclaimed with a little bounce. It was rare that Anne got to get out totally alone, but when she could, she treated herself – it was a woman's prerogative and practically a cardinal rule to have a haircut or a manicure if she could afford it and some much needed down time.

"Excellent! You want the usual?" Anne really did have a regular haircut, even though she had tried something new last month.

"I think just a shampoo and a trim this time." She sat back in the chair and Lisa went to work. Raheleh was outside with the broom sweeping the walk and Damien was on his lunch break; Allison wasn't scheduled today, and it was just her and Lisa in the shop. They gossiped like a couple of old hats.

"Who's the new girl?" Anne asked.

"That's Raheleh," Lisa replied. "She does 'good business.'" She tried to imitate Raheleh's accent and felt kind of bad for making fun. "Ok, no really, she's alright. I've got another one too, Allison." Anne hadn't met her yet, and wouldn't today.

"What's she like?" Anne asked. Lisa thought for a moment.

"She's nice. She's a little older than me, and has a couple of kids. Her boyfriend is from the UK, and her ex-husband is sort of a drunk. She's not a bad stylist at all. Reliable and honest, at least." Lisa had told Anne about Angelica and Gabriella. Lisa dumped shampoo into her palm and massaged Anne's scalp with it. Anne sank into the seat and her body relaxed.

"When are you bringing in the kids for a haircut?" Lisa asked Anne. The thought terrified Anne, really. Karl and Robbie were ok, and Erik, of course, wouldn't really need a haircut for a while, but Ieva had trouble sitting still and Anne was worried. Ieva didn't like the smock or the scissors, and the noises scared her so giving her the simplest haircut was difficult.

"I don't know," she said to Lisa apprehensively. Lisa stopped working and leaned down so that she could see Anne's face. She already knew Anne's mind.

"Stop fretting. We can accommodate her. I have a *lot* of clients with sensory issues; I've got a special drape for the chair so it looks inviting. You can come after hours so there is no noise and I'll play Ieva's favorite Disney music. I'll do it myself and I promise that if we have a problem, I'll cut Karl and Robbie *and you,* for free." Anne sighed again. Nothing was better than a hairdresser that could please.

"We'll see," was all she said, and Lisa nodded firmly behind her. Just then, Raheleh walked through the door, dragging a gentleman in behind her. She was holding his hand.

"You need a good haircut. Come in, I give it to you." Raheleh caressed his arm sweetly. Lisa wanted to crawl under the table; the man that she was dragging into the salon was the landlord.

"Hi, Charles," Lisa said to him. She glared at Raheleh. "*Mr. Wilson* doesn't need a haircut; he's here to collect the rent, as he is the *landlord.*" Lisa said this through gritted teeth and tried to get across to Raheleh that she was doing something wrong. Charles was nice, and surely wouldn't throw her out.

"Well, Pearl would tell me that I do need a haircut," he said sadly. He ran his fingers through his whitening hair. Lisa felt bad for Mr. Wilson in that moment.

"Good, Pearl is smart woman, you sit." Raheleh demanded, pushing him down into the chair. Lisa's stomach clenched. Pearl had passed away a short while ago and Charles had taken over her properties. She prayed Raheleh wouldn't say anything else. She exchanged a look with Anne as she rinsed the other woman's hair. Lisa grabbed a fluffy white towel and jokingly threw it over the top of Anne's head before drying it off. She leaned down and whispered in Anne's ear.

"Don't leave, I might need a witness." Anne nodded and settled down in the chair. Lisa handed her a magazine and Anne eavesdropped from behind it. Lisa walked to her office and pulled the money that she owed the landlord out of her expense envelope. When she walked it back out there, Raheleh was putting a smock on "Mister Wilson," and getting him ready for a cut. There was no way Lisa was letting his name slip now that Raheleh was paying so much more attention.

"How are you, Mr. Wilson?" she asked him. He sighed.

"Getting better," he said to her. "It's been hard. We've got most of the properties switched over, and the bank said that I can sell some of them. I sold the clubs to Amy Pozner when Pearl started getting sick. One of them is going for 1.6 million and it's got a golf course attached to it." Raheleh's eyes grew big.

"You have lots of money. This Pearl, she is your wife?" she asked bluntly. Charles shifted in his seat and looked uncomfortably at Lisa. Lisa jammed her eyes shut in sympathy and looked distraught. Charles just shook his head.

"Was. Pearl died a couple of months ago." Raheleh's eyes grew as big as saucers.

"You are single?" she said to him. "And you have so much money!! You should go out with me." She leaned down so that her breasts touched his shoulders and massaged the back of his neck.

"I give you good haircut." She said to him. "You need new wife." Charles looked at Lisa and started to get up but Raheleh pushed him back in the chair.

"Oh –*kay*, Raheleh, I don't think Mr. Wilson needs a haircut today." She muscled Raheleh out the way and Raheleh glared at her. Charles pulled off the smock and looked relieved, and Lisa wasn't sure but she thought she saw tears welling up in his eyes as he stood up. Charles had loved Pearl, and they were good together. Lisa knew them well, and it was Pearl that had offered her the property – they also owned Jacob's place, and knew that Lisa would be a good tenant. Charles left the shop. Anne put her magazine down and Lisa threw her another towel. Anne dried her hair and smiled at Lisa, encouraging the young woman.

"It'll be ok, and I'll be back." Anne said to her. Lisa hugged her and whispered thanks in her ear before she left.

A month passed and then blurred into six. Damien and Raheleh were still bickering in the back of the shop, but it was tolerable. Allison was working three days a week and her boys were doing well in school. One afternoon, she came to work with red, puffy eyes and tears rolling down her face.

"What's wrong?" Lisa asked. Allison frowned.

"I had to take Dylan to soccer practice this afternoon, and David isn't answering the phone so he can go pick him up. I've been calling all morning."

"Do you need to leave? I can hold it down here."

"No, I called the one of the other moms and she's going to pick him up. I'm fine. I'm a little worried about David, though. He didn't answer yesterday, either. I don't know what's going on." She looked tired.

"Well, let's try and make it through this day, and it will be alright, I'm sure." Lisa wasn't quite sure what to say. She didn't have to say much, because just then, Damien walked out of the back room, wiping his hands on a towel.

"Someone called today from another salon looking for a job,"

50

he said. "You were at lunch."

"Called from another salon? You mean like a competitor?"

"Yea, said his name was Vince, or something like that."

"I'll check him out. Did he leave a message?"

"Said he would be back," Damien said uninterestedly. Lisa scowled. Another long day was passing. The sun in the windows grew long and the business slowed down. She had locked the doors and was counting the tickets when she heard a knock at the barber shop door. She looked up and saw that it was Allison, rapping frantically on the door. Lisa opened the door and let her in; Allison dissolved in Lisa's arms.

"Oh my God, Lisa. We went over there. We went there. He was dead in the floor." Lisa's mouth dropped open and she put her arms around the obviously upset girl.

"Who? What happened?" Allison tried to compose herself. She sniffed deeply and looked at Lisa.

"Dylan and I went to David's house to see if he was home or if he was going to go to Dylan's game tomorrow, or find out why he wasn't answering his phone. I knocked and no one answered, so I knocked again, and his car was in the driveway so I checked the door. Dylan had to call the police, and when they came, they broke down the door. Lisa it was awful, there was this awful smell. The police found him dead in the back room, covered in vomit and blood. They said that he had been there for a while, days or even possibly a week. I was there for hours with the police." Lisa was astonished. She put her arms around the other woman.

"What are you going to do?" Lisa asked.

"I need a couple of days off to take care of things," she said tearfully.

"Take as long as you need, Allison, I'm sorry this is just awful."

"Ok. I think it should be about a week."

"That's fine. I got a call today from another stylist – are you going to be upset if I hire him to replace you while you're gone? We could use the extra hands when you come back." Lisa didn't want to upset Allison any more than she already was. Allison nodded at her.

"Ok, I still have a job when I get back, right?" She looked nervous.

"Yes, of course!" Lisa exclaimed. "Just come back when you're ready." Allison hugged her tight and turned to leave. Lisa locked the door behind her and finished closing up the salon. It had been a long day.

The next morning she got a call from the stylist that Damien had said called earlier that week.

"Is this Lisa?" A strange voice came over the line. He sounded like he was Italian.

"Yes, this is Lisa," she replied. "May I ask who this is?"

"This is Vincenzo, I called earlier to ask about a job."

"Yes, Damien told me. Are you currently working?"

"I am, but I need a side job."

"Oh, where do you work?"

"I work at Shear Madness." Shear Madness was a salon that was just a few doors down from Lisa. The owner was a fat bellied balding stump of a man that wore loud shirts and drove a loud car. He wore pinky rings and smoked big stinky cigars. He cut TV hair.

"If you already work for a stylist, why do you want to work for me?" Lisa asked cautiously. She wasn't going to hire someone that already had a job as a stylist.

"The checks from Shear Madness bounce. I have to go to the bank he cuts them on and make sure they have the money on the account. Plus, the owner is a slave driver; he gets uptight during lunch breaks and doesn't want to let anyone even go to the bathroom." Lisa rolled her eyes; he was probably exaggerating.

"Well, I could use someone to come in and cut hair while my other stylist is on sabbatical."

"I'm free. He's cutting our hours back to two days a week because he can hardly afford to stay open."

"Come in this afternoon." Lisa hung up with him and the afternoon passed. When she heard a knock at her back door, she confusedly opened it to see a dark skinned, dark haired gentleman standing there. He was wearing pants that were a little too tight and his shirt was stretched over his belly just a hair, but he was still pretty good looking. He grabbed her hand.

"You must be the beautiful Lisa." He said to her, kissing the back of her hand lightly.

"I'm just Lisa, but yes," she said modestly. "You must be Vinny." Of course he was.

"Oh yes, I am." She walked away from him, turning back that so she could retreat into the salon. He followed her.

"I love this place!" he said to her, turning around in the main work area. She had done well with what she had on the ground floor of her building. It wasn't a huge salon – in the front she had room for three chairs, and they all doubled as coloring stations so there wasn't anything that couldn't be done in this area of the salon. Since she had already sectioned off a chair into the stock room again for Damien, she had replaced it out front so she had four. There were only two other rooms, one of which was occupied by Damien during his hours, and one that held her office. The salon also had a tiny bathroom with a little sink.

Still, Lisa had done her best. It was free of dust and there was no grime. The walls were painted a cheery white and the hardwood floors were stained a nice light brown. There was a table with some magazines in one corner, and a few toys in a little bin. There were posters on the wall of men and women with the latest styles, and a couple of inspirational bits sprinkled here and there. The stations were clean and organized when Vincenzo saw them, and even though Raheleh gave Damien a hard time, she at least appreciated that he could *try* and clean up.

"Thanks, Vinny. I can set you up over here," she said, pointing at Allison's station. It was stocked and ready for her, but she wouldn't be back for a little while. Vincenzo sat down in one of the chairs and wriggled his butt in the chair.

"Only the best for Lisa's customers, yea? This is wonderful!" he exclaimed, jumping out of the seat.

"Well, you're on duty today. Damien will be back in a little while, and then he'll be here till four. You'll stay with me till about seven." Customers were already obliging Vincenzo's appearance by coming into the salon. First a lady, and then a man; Vincenzo greeted them both with great big smiles and seated them each in a chair. Lisa smiled at Vincenzo and walked around to tend the other customer. They worked together, chatting. She found out a lot about Vincenzo that day; besides being a good hair stylist, he was a flirt, an avid coffee drinker and a foodie at heart. A spirited conversation about spaghetti turned into an all over rant from Vincenzo.

"You *cannot* put canned spaghetti sauce on pasta and make it taste good."

"Chef Boyardee did it," said the customer in Lisa's chair. Vincenzo dropped the scissors and threw his hand over his eyes.

"Chef who?" said Vincenzo. "That fat cartoon of a chef is the worst tragedy to ever cross the line of Italian cooking. You don't put good food in a can unless you're going to feed it to your dog. You need fresh tomatoes; quality meat, good herbs, and you must cook over a gas stove if you're presented with the opportunity."

"Vinny, you sound like you know what you're talking about," said Lisa. "Are you as good a cook as you are a hairdresser?" She was in the middle of a haircut herself. Vincenzo picked up the scissors and gave them a rinse before drying them off and continuing his job on the gentleman in the chair.

"Beautiful Lisa, I am a better chef than I am anything. Which is saying a lot because I am good at everything I do." Vincenzo, that braggart. He was going to do just fine, Lisa thought as her clients chuckled at him appreciatively.

"How do you cook so good?" she asked him.

"I charm old women into giving me their secrets," he laughed. Lisa wondered if it weren't true.

"Do you ever visit that little deli on Pine Street?" Vincenzo's client asked him.

"No, that's just a sandwich shop. It's good in a pinch," he said shrugging. "Every Saturday I take the train to the Bronx and visit Joe's Italian Deli on Arthur Avenue. They make the best homemade mozzarella you can buy, and they are the only ones that have my veal."

"You make veal?" asked Lisa. She *did* like Italian food, after all.

"No, I make meatballs out of beef and veal with just a bit of pork. They are to die for!" He kissed his fingertips and shook his hand at them. Vincenzo was so dramatic.

"What kind of sauce do you buy for them?" asked Lisa's client, who was almost done with her cut. Vincenzo shook his head and wandered over to her chair, getting close to her. She was completely under Vincenzo's spell.

"You are *bellissima, mio amore,* but you know nothing about food." Vincenzo grabbed her hand and kissed it the same way he had kissed Lisa's hand and she blushed. Lisa laughed at him and slapped his hand away.

"What, you are jealous, yes?" he asked, kissing Lisa on the cheek and floating back to the man in the chair. He was nearly done; all Vincenzo had to do was comb him and dust him off before sending him out to the street. He left Vincenzo a five dollar tip. Lisa smiled. Now let's hope he had the same effect on Raheleh and Damien. Time would tell, and it did.

As it turns out, food wasn't the only thing that Vincenzo was passionate about. He loved his coffee too. Every morning on his way to work, he would stop by Dunkin Donuts and pick Lisa up a cup of coffee and bring doughnuts or crullers for whoever worked. When he took his break before lunch he would jog past Bruegger's Bagels to see who was working on his way to Starbucks. He would always come back with an extra coffee for Lisa and a funny anecdote about what girl was working that day. He was a good tipper; Lisa often wondered how he was able to afford all of these amenities when he was working two jobs. One day, she asked him.

"I'm a millionaire," Vincenzo said simply, shrugging. Lisa had heard some stories from him but this was one that she thought was farfetched.

"Yea right!" she exclaimed, snorting. Vincenzo smiled and pulled his wallet out, fishing in it until he found a crinkled piece of news print. Lisa opened it up, and there was Vincenzo's face, beaming next to a little bald man in a three piece suit, the two of them holding a fake five million dollar check. The caption read "Vincenzo Romano, winner of the Connecticut Lottery, shown here with officiators." Vincenzo was loaded.

"Why do you even work?" Lisa asked incredulously.

"Why not, I have nothing better to do. My wife took all my money and moved it into a trust account so I wouldn't gamble it all away."

"Smart move…" Lisa murmured.

"I won't disagree," he said amicably. "She knows me well." It was nearing the end of his shift, and Raheleh would be coming in behind him. Allison had been out for almost a week and had called to ask for just a little longer. Vincenzo was doing well, and Damien, of course, was Damien. As Vincenzo kissed her goodbye, she waited for Raheleh to come in so that she could go to lunch. Damien was just coming out of the backroom with the broom, sweeping a pile of clippings out into the main floor, and then closing the door behind him. He left the pile there and walked around to get the corners of room and swept that debris toward his pile. He often did that – came around with the broom to catch the whole floor when he came out of his stockroom. There was nothing wrong with what he was doing. Raheleh didn't agree, and before she had even greeted anyone, she was on top of Damien.

"You missed a spot," she said, pointing at the pile. "You just leave this mess here for someone to track around?"

"Who told you to come in here and start bossing me?" Damien snapped. He wasn't wearing his glasses, and to Lisa, that was a bad sign. It meant that he was probably in a mood. Lisa bit her lip, and Raheleh of course, continued.

"I told you, you are terrible," she hissed. She strode over to Damien and tried to snatch the broom from him.

"Get the hell away from me, lady!" He pulled the broom away from her and she let go of it, falling over backwards. She started to writhe on the floor, screaming.

"Kill me! He is trying to kill me! Please! Bring my medication, please!" Lisa's mouth fell open and she looked at Damien incredulously. He dropped the broom and held his hands out, eyes wide. Raheleh was having a royal fit. Damien panicked and grabbed the phone, ready to call 911. Lisa bent over Raheleh, who stood up screaming, a long wail of apparent pain caught in her throat. She ran over to Damien and slapped the receiver out of his hands and then clutched at his shirt. Damien backed off a few steps, trying to get away from her. He looked to Lisa for help. She grabbed Raheleh by the arm and dragged her outside.

"You can't be doing this in my shop." Raheleh continued to kick and scream. When Lisa had her outside, Raheleh slammed her head into the sidewalk and let out a piercing shriek. Lisa tried to help her off the sidewalk and she refused rolling away from her.

"My medication, please!" Raheleh kicked her feet and slammed her head into the walk again.

"Raheleh please, this is my business, get up," she said, stomping her foot at Raheleh.

"Please, bring my pills, please, bring my medication," she was still on the ground and showed no sign of getting up.

"You know what?" Lisa said to Raheleh in desperation. "There is nothing wrong with you. You're fired. Get your things and get out of my shop before I call the cops." Lisa turned and went back inside. Lisa finally had Raheleh's attention.

"Wait, please!" she said, her thick accent hoarse and gritty. Lisa closed the door of the shop behind her, and Raheleh followed. Damien had retreated back into the stock room.

"I said to clean out your station and leave." Lisa wasn't kidding, nor was she playing. She'd had enough.

"But I bring good business."

"No, you don't. You," Lisa paused. She had almost said that Raheleh was an embarrassment, but Lisa's tact kicked in just time.

"You just need to go. I can't have someone working here that is as unstable as you are."

"Please, I need this job."

"There are other salons."

"Please I cut good hair." Big fat tears started to fall from Raheleh's eyes.

"No. I can't have someone working here that is as unstable as you are. Forget it. You're fired." Raheleh cleaned out her station, the whole time muttering under her breath in a language that Lisa did not understand. She left, but not before she approached Lisa again.

"You are making big mistake," she said to Lisa. "I do good business."

"I can't have someone working here that's going to beat their head on the side walk. You gotta go." Lisa shook her head.

"Big mistake," said Raheleh. She left the shop, and Lisa was standing there. There were two customers ready for cuts that had witnessed the whole thing. She knocked on the stockroom door. Damien opened it a crack and then all the way when he saw it wasn't Raheleh.

"She gone?" he asked her warily.

"Yep."

"Good, she-"

"Don't even say it, or you're fired." Lisa turned on her heel and put all of her energy and attention on her customers. She sent one to Damien's station in the back and concentrated on the other. Another long day was passing. At lunch time, Anne came in with Karl and Robbie. Lisa pounced on them immediately. Damien was working a split shift and wouldn't be back for a little while.

"Hey guys!" she said to them, winking at Anne while she pointedly pretended to ignore her. "Coming to get a haircut?"

"Yes, ma'am," they chorused together. Lisa smiled at Anne, impressed. They were so cute and so polite. She looked at Anne.

"You didn't bring her?" she asked, smiling still. Anne shook her head.

"I'm not ready yet," Anne smiled back. She knew Lisa would understand.

"Well, it's alright; we'll get around to it. Have a seat mama, and I'll get some stuff that we pull out for the kids." Lisa fished out a special smock printed with teddy bears and balloons. It had a Velcro neck and snaps just in case. She pulled out a drape for the chair – really just an old sheet – with cartoon characters on it and threw it over the seat. It suddenly looked like a fun place to get a haircut instead of a stodgy old barber chair. The oldest of the boys, Robbie, ran up to Lisa.

"I want to go first!" he shouted at her, gleefully.

"Robbie!" Anne said sternly. Robbie turned around with a guilty look.

"It's ok mama," said Lisa. "He's just excited about that chair, is all. Come on, babe." Lisa pointed at the chair and Robbie

58

hopped in it, ready for his haircut. She looked at Anne while she worked on Robbie. He was flaxen haired, like his brother. Anne wasn't exactly a blonde, but she wanted blonde hair so she colored it when she felt like it.

"I had to fire Raheleh today," she said as she sprayed Robbie's hair. Anne cocked her head at Lisa.

"Really, what happened?" she asked curiously.

"Lady went berserk and ran out of the shop screaming. I wanted to die and melt into the sidewalk." Anne's eyebrows rose comically in surprise.

"Stop it!" exclaimed Anne. "Kidding, right?"

"You wish."

"So what now?" Anne wondered sometimes how Lisa did it all. Lisa shook her head and started snipping away at Robbie's hair. He was being a little angel in the chair and wasn't giving Lisa a lick of trouble.

"Well, I've still got Damien." She looked dolefully at the stockroom door. Anne smiled at her. She had heard and seen some things with Damien, too.

"Allison should be coming back any time, and I've got this guy Tommy that comes in on Saturdays. I still have Vinny when he's on hiatus from next door, and then there's me, of course, so I mean, it will be alright." Lisa shrugged. Robbie was done and she leaned down to have a look at him and spun him in the pretty chair. She handed him a mirror. Admiring himself, he gave it back to her, beaming. Lisa held up a lollipop and waggled her eyebrows at him. Karl jumped out of his seat.

"My turn!" he said, running up to Lisa.

"Karl!" said Anne. Lisa shook her head.

"Come on, guy," Lisa said to Karl. Karl sat just as still. Lisa swung the cover around him and started spraying his hair down with water to make it easier to cut. He giggled in the chair. Lisa wondered how Anne did it.

"How do you do it, Anne? How do you chase after all of these kids?"

"What do you mean?"

"I mean, gosh. You have four babies!"

59

"I don't know. You just sorta do it. I mean, I do a lot of volunteer work for organizations that advocate for children with disabilities. Sometimes they have family events or playgroups that we participate in. Ieva is a handful but she's also so adorable. We have a lot of therapy appointments that are enjoyable for both of us. We have a good time!" Anne shrugged.

"It sounds like a lot of fun. I know me and Larry were talking about what we would do if I got pregnant. He said he'd have to make me an honest woman. I'm not against it." She wouldn't know that in the next few months he would ask her to marry him and they would elope to Niagara Falls without telling her mother or anyone else.

"It is fun, sometimes." Anne didn't know how else to describe what she did. She had her kids. In another life, she had been an attorney with a practice in the Bronx. Arnie's job had made him a little well off, so there was no need for her to work if she didn't want to. They were by no means without. She was educated, wealthy, and well-traveled; now, she was more full of life than she had ever been doing any of those things, just by staying home with her children. Best of all, she had could afford a nanny for the three boys while she concentrated on her daughter's care. Ieva and Karl and Robbie were all good kids, and she was sure Erik would prove to be good too. It was a good life. Lisa tried to hand Karl the mirror and he waved her off.

"I know it looks good!" he said, hopping down from the chair and going to stand by his mom. Lisa looked at him incredulously. He shrugged her and grinned. Lisa was lost to his charms. His hair, after all, *did* look good.

CHAPTER 7:
THE NO GOOD VERY BAD WEEK

"I'm serious, Mom, she literally beat her head against the ground." Lisa was on the phone with her mother after work on the evening that she had fired Raheleh. She frightened Damien so badly that he told me he was turning in his notice next week."

"That's not safe at all! What kind of unhinged people do you have working for you?" Lisa's mother was a chronic worrier.

"It's fine, Mom."

"Well, you should come stay here tonight." Lisa sighed.

"Would it make you feel better?"

"Yes, of course."

"What about Larry?"

"He'll live. You can call him at work and let him know." Lisa smiled. There was no arguing with her mother.

"Alright then." Lisa hung up with her mother and gathered up an overnight bag. She drove over there and the rest of the night passed uneventfully. In the morning, Lisa was getting her coffee ready when she saw a woman dressed in black, marching up and down in front of her mother's house. Raheleh. Lisa looked at her mother.

"What is that?" she asked Lisa. The woman was dressed in black from head to toe, wearing a thick veil and long sleeves. She was walking back and forth in front of her mother's house, waving her arms. She would bend down and touch the ground, putting her face to the pavement, wailing at the top of her lungs as though someone had died.

"That is Raheleh." Lisa said, pointedly. She was angry. There was no possible way that Raheleh could have found her here – her mother had an unlisted number and was not in the phone books anywhere. Lisa had heard that you could look on the internet to find out phone numbers but they were few and far between. The internet was still brand new and surely the information superhighway hadn't found her just yet. There was no possible way she could have found them unless Raheleh had followed Lisa from her house. "Wild woman," Lisa muttered to herself before stepping out of the door. She went right up to Raheleh.

"What is *wrong* with you?" Lisa asked her.

"Miss Lisa, please give Raheleh a second chance. I do good business for you. I cut good hair. Please give me a second chance." Lisa blew a noise out of her lips and looked at Raheleh.

"Is this a joke? I would never hire you again." Lisa was losing her temper and was sick of Raheleh. "Take off," she told the other woman.

"You'll regret this," Raheleh sniffed.

"I don't care." Lisa shrugged and went back inside. Her mother was at her heels.

"Do you think we should call the police?" Raheleh was leaving, and Lisa was relieved.

"Nah, just let her go. I don't think we'll hear anymore from her." Lisa kissed her mother on the cheek and left for the shop. She was greeted by the phone ringing.

"Hello?"

"Hey, Lisa, it's me, Allison!" Right on time, as usual, thought Lisa.

"Hey! How's it going?" Lisa asked her.

"Good. Are you ready for me?"

"More than ever, when are you coming back?"

"I'm free this week."

"Excellent, we need you. I had to fire someone, and we've got two new hairdressers, but we still need you."

"Alright!"

"Can you come in this afternoon?"

"Absolutely."

"Are you ok? Really?"

"Yea…we got the house cleaned out and we're moving into it this weekend."

"Wait, what?" Lisa was confused. They were moving into the house that her ex-husband had died in?

"Yea. The house was entrusted to the boys and it's already paid for, so we're moving in." Lisa was grossed out, but whatever. It wasn't her, what did she care.

"Well that's...good," said Lisa noncommittally. Allison didn't seem to notice, so Lisa didn't press. They agreed for Allison to come in that afternoon to take over Raheleh's shift. She would be working with Vincenzo, and it was Damien's day off. Lisa went to lunch that afternoon with a bit of a bounce in her step. She walked down to the deli to order a sandwich and was shocked to see what had come back to. Lisa kept her car in a parking garage close to the salon and walked from there. It was only a block or two, and it kept her car out of the tiny lot out front. She was still talking to the police when Allison pulled up into the nearby parking lot that afternoon.

"Lisa, is everything alright?" Allison hustled to get out of her car and went to hug Lisa. Lisa halfheartedly put an arm around her and patted her. She looked like she had been crying. "What happened?" Allison cried.

"I went to lunch and I came back and my car was torn up." Allison looked over at the parking lot, and there was Lisa's car, covered in pink and black spray paint from one end to other. It had been defaced, and written on in a different language that Allison couldn't read. Lisa shook her head. The policeman talking to her took her hand and patted it.

"We'll find out more about it," he said to her. Lisa sniffed.

"I already know who it is," she told him. "I fired Raheleh yesterday and she was at my mother's house this morning, asking for her job back. She threatened me when I wouldn't give it to her."

"That isn't proof, Lisa."

"Look at my car!" Lisa cried. It was written all over in Persian, Raheleh's native language.

"We still have to investigate, ma'am." He patted her hand again and released it, waving over another officer. He advised the policeman to beef up security at the lot and told Lisa that it was

63

safe to go back to work. Lisa looked down at her lunch and handed it to Allison.

"Here. I don't have an appetite anymore." She glumly marched to the salon, leaving Allison to follow her.

"Well, I'll just save it for her," Allison said to herself, hurrying behind Lisa. When she got to the shop, Vincenzo greeted Lisa.

"Bella, are you alright? What happened? Who do I have to kill?" Lisa couldn't help but laugh, but the air was still serious. She told Vincenzo what happened. Damien nodded and pursed his lips, looking Lisa in the eye. Damien knew who had defaced her car, too, but wisely said nothing.

"Vinny," Lisa sighed wearily. "Stop." Vincenzo snorted.

"Fine. But you just give me the word, and I'll solve the problem for you." He kissed both of Lisa's hands and then realized Allison was there too. He walked around her and viewed her from every angle. When he came around to face her, she was frowning.

"Hello, beautiful," he said to her. She sniffed at him disdainfully and looked at him like he was covered in bugs.

"Hi," was all she replied. Lisa smelled trouble, and intervened.

"Vinny, this is Allison, Allison, this is my other hairdresser, Vincenzo." Vincenzo bowed low to Allison tried to take her hand to kiss it. She snatched her hand away and shook her head.

"No, please, thank you," she said politely. Vincenzo straightened up and looked as if he had been slapped.

"You don't like me?" he asked with some incredulity. Allison just shook her head and addressed Lisa.

"Where to, boss lady?" Lisa smiled and pointed at Raheleh's station, which Lisa had already had cleaned out and ready for Allison. She was next to Vincenzo, who was doing his best to charm the pants off of her. It wasn't working; it seemed that Allison was immune to his Italian charm. He tried to talk to her about food; it didn't work. He tried to talk to her about hair; that didn't work either. He flirted with her, and when that didn't work, he gave up talking to her altogether unless he absolutely had to. Allison didn't like Vincenzo at all, and she made clear to Lisa after about a week.

"Lisa, you really hired that pig?" Lisa looked up from her papers. Christina was blunt and Lisa knew that she wouldn't hold back her opinion, but that was pretty inappropriate.

"What?"

"Where did you find Vinny, in the dumpster behind the Italian Deli?"

"Allison!"

"I'm sorry, he's just disgusting; the way he butters up all the women and then talks to their men like he's never said a word, that's ridiculous. Then he thinks he knows everything about cutting hair and coloring? He makes me feel like he knows better than everyone." Allison snorted and shook her head. Lisa shrugged.

"I need people that are going to cut hair. No one complained when you left to go take care of your family, so now that you're back, I'd appreciate it if you wouldn't complain about whom I hire." Lisa hadn't meant to be harsh, but there it was. She was tired of the drama already. Lisa pushed her chair back, and Allison just shook her head, muttered as she followed Lisa out of the office. Damien was in, Vincenzo was in. Tommy the Marine would be in later. The atmosphere was thick, as usual. When she came out of her office Vincenzo was telling a story, and Allison was listening with her nose curled up. Damien was holed up in the stockroom as usual, but he had the door open, which meant that he was listening to Vincenzo's story, too.

"I got right in his face," he said to the customer. "I told him, 'you don't care about the education of students, you want them to be stupid like you." Vincenzo was inches away from the customer, but the client was listening intently.

"Well she was only a day late, I don't see the big deal," said the client.

"Yea, but a day late is a day late," said the practical Allison.

"Doesn't matter," said Vincenzo. "No one treats my daughter like a common pig."

"Must run in the family," muttered Allison. If Vincenzo heard her, he pretended not to.

"Anyway, I protect my children, and I'm not afraid-a no body." Vincenzo snapped his fingers. Allison rolled her eyes and

65

looked towards Lisa, who was standing by Damien's door. Damien shut the door. Lisa sighed. Just another day in paradise. Vincenzo's phone rang as his client was exiting the shop so he took the call right there in the shop.

"Mama!" he cried into the phone. He began to speak in fluent and rapid Italian. He stopped and listened and then the smile ran away from his face.

"Son of a bitch," he said into the phone, frowning. Lisa looked around at the clients, and mouthed an apology.

"Vinny," she said warningly. Vincenzo wasn't there he was in his conversation. Allison sniffed, and Damien's door opened just a crack. Vincenzo went back to speaking Italian, alternately cursing. When he began yelling into the phone, Lisa walked up to him and snapped her fingers in his face, making a slashing motion around her throat to tell him to end the call. He nodded to her

"I gotta go back to work, Mama," he said to her. "Love you."

"Vinny," Lisa started.

"*Bella,* I am so sorry. That was Mama, she gets me so mad." Lisa knew, it wasn't a rare occurrence for Vincenzo to lose his temper with whoever was on the phone. This was the first time however, he had used foul language on the cutting floor. He kissed Lisa on the cheek.

"Forgive me?" Allison looked hopeful for a moment.

"Of course, Vinny, just watch your mouth." Lisa turned around just in time to see Allison frown. She was hoping for something more, but it wasn't coming. Disappointment shone all over her face. "And no more calls on the salon floor. Take it to the back." Lisa gave Allison that one as a freebie. What could she say, she was a softie.

The afternoon came and went. Vincenzo left them, and it was Lisa and Allison in the shop. They were closing; Lisa was in her office counting money and ticking off checkmarks on a list with her supplies on it. Allison was out on the salon floor, giving each chair a final wipe down, then preparing the whole floor for a sweep and mop. Lisa wasn't quite able to afford a cleaning crew yet, so everyone did their part. Lisa dropped her pen when Allison shouted her name from the cutting floor. Rushing out to the door, she saw Allison pointing at the station underneath where Vincenzo usually worked. There were boxes on the floor; Allison had been putting up supplies.

"Tell me that's not what I think it is," cried Allison, pointing. Lisa couldn't see what she was pointing at, so she bent down and peered into the cubby hole.

"Be careful, boss lady!!" Allison shrieked. Lisa backed up a step expecting to find a mouse or some kind of snake in the building. What she found instead was a 9mm semiautomatic handgun, hidden among the boxes of color in a bundle of Lisa's old salon towels. Lisa was stunned. She straightened up, not looking at Allison.

"Christ. Um. Ok. Um. Right. Damn." She gathered up the bundle, towels and all, and took it into her office. Allison followed her.

"What are you going to do? Do you think it's stolen?"

"No, he can afford it, but he's not going to leave it in my salon. Go ahead and finish up. I'll handle it."

"Hey, I heard that he was on the wrong side of Colton King and that King had a vendetta against him for working for someone else and that Vincenzo owed him money." Allison shrugged. Lisa shook her head. She sounded gleeful. Inside Lisa churned. What was she going to do? What would Orv do? Good old Orv…man to man he would tell him to take his pea shooter and put it where the sun don't shine, but most of all to get it the hell out of his barber shop. Whether or not Vincenzo had a job after that depended on how well Vincenzo took it.

Allison backed out of Lisa's office and went back out to the floor. She finished stocking boxes and supplies and was sweeping the floor. As she got out the mop bucket, Lisa waved her off and told her to skip it. She called Vincenzo and asked him to come in the next day before anyone else got there. When she heard the knock at the back door, she unlocked it without opening it and Vincenzo came in without preamble. He followed her into the office. She didn't hesitate. Lisa contemplated pointing the gun at him and asking him about it, but she wasn't sure it wasn't loaded so she nixed the idea.

"Vinny, what the hell is this?"

"Bella, I'm so sorry. I thought that after all of the problems this week, we could all use a little protection here at the salon."

"I heard that you've got some problems with Colton King," she said bluntly. "If that's the case, then you probably shouldn't work here."

"No, mio amore, please. You misunderstand. I would never use this in anger at anyone." He picked up the pistol and unloaded it on her desk. She jumped every time a bullet hit the table top.

"We needed the extra security," he explained. "Can I just take it home?"

"Please, and don't bring the damned thing back. What were you *thinking?*" she asked him.

"I was just sure that we needed some security. Yes, I have trouble with King, too, but that woman…" He was talking about Raheleh, she knew. Lisa nodded her head.

"I know, but let the cops do their job," she said to him. Vincenzo nodded.

"Are you going to fire me?" he asked her. Lisa sighed.

"I can't right now. I need you. This is your one and only second chance. Allison wants me to fire you outright." Vincenzo nodded. He looked sad.

"I'm sorry, beautiful. Forgive me?"

"Of course, Vinny. Now get." She waved him off and he left. The same morning, Anne brought her husband into the shop for the first time. He was paunchy and balding, as though his hours on the golf course hadn't done him any good. He was thinning on top, but Lisa didn't say anything about that. Anne introduced him.

"Lisa, this is my husband, Arnie. He wanted to see where this place was and see about a haircut." Lisa smiled at him and Arnie nodded. She gestured to the chair.

"Would you like to sit down?" she asked him.

"No, I'll wait for someone else. Do you have any men that work here?" Anne's mouth dropped open a little and the effect wasn't lost on Lisa. Anne snapped her lips closed and frowned at him behind his back. Lisa shrugged and smiled at Arnie, pretending that she hadn't seen it; the last thing she wanted to do

68

was alienate her favorite client and her husband.

"Damien will be here in a little bit," she confirmed. It was that simple. Arnie looked around at Anne.

"If it's all the same, I'll just leave you here and go out for a while till he gets here." Anne nodded and Arnie left the salon. He would come again in the future, when Damien was there. As it happened, he was as much of a regular as Anne was, but he never brought the kids nor let Lisa cut his hair.

"Really?" Lisa said to her when Arnie was gone.

"Yea, sorry." Anne said. Lisa shrugged again, patting her shoulder. Anne sat in the chair and leaned back. "The usual, if you don't mind." Lisa already knew what Anne wanted. She was here often. As Lisa threw the smock around her neck, Anne looked towards the big window out front.

"So when did you decide to put in cameras?"

"What do you mean?" Lisa was confused. She had no need for security cameras, despite all that had gone on, especially with Vincenzo and his pistol.

"There are guys outside installing cameras facing your doors." Lisa dropped what she was doing with Anne and poked her head out the door. Sure enough, there was an installer screwing in the camera. The wires were hanging there by the wall unplugged into anything as of yet.

"What are you doing? You can't point those at my salon."

"They were ordered by the salon next door."

"Well point them somewhere else."

"I'll point them where I was told by the person who paid me."

"Colton King." It wasn't a question, and when he nodded, she let the door go and went back inside to Anne. Lisa was furious.

"What's wrong?" Anne asked.

"They're putting cameras up on my salon."

"Who!?"

"Shear Madness."

"Bullcrap."

"No, really." Anne's eyes widened. Lisa nodded at her.

"This has something to do with Vinny." Lisa said to her. She was quiet for the rest of the haircut and Anne didn't press her. She

69

was in a mood for the rest of the afternoon. She didn't approach Vincenzo and when Damien came in that afternoon, she shut his stock room door on him before he had the chance to. Damien was surprised, but knew better than to ask. It was that afternoon that Allison approached Lisa for the final time. Allison noticed the cameras too, and asked Lisa about them. Lisa explained what was going on, and Allison frowned.

"We have to talk," Allison began. Lisa thought she knew what was coming.

"Go ahead. Sit down." Lisa told her. She sat back in her chair while Allison seated herself in the folding chair across from her desk.

"Well, I think I'm going to find another place to work," she said tentatively. She handed Lisa a piece of paper; it was a two week notice.

"Is it because of Vinny? I can't lose either one of you right now, Allison." Lisa knew that Allison found him distasteful, but if it came down to Allison quitting, it was easier to tell Vincenzo to behave himself than it was to find another hairdresser.

"Well, it doesn't help, but it's nothing here that would make me leave like that. You know I would complain to you first if it were really Vinny. He's a jerk, but so what? You have to roll with the punches, sometimes. I mean…the gun thing was scary, but I've heard stories about Colton King, and I'd carry a gun if I were on the wrong side of him too. I'd have already fired his tail because of his mouth, but that's not my business. Actually, the problem is that the boys are starting to act out at home. I can't leave them with their stepdad anymore, and the school called today saying that I needed to make an appointment for a conference with the guidance counselors, so I have no idea what's going on with them."

"So you would leave anyway," Lisa said bluntly. She liked Allison but it sounded like she had a lot on her plate right now. "Do you already have another job?" Allison nodded.

"Sorta. I applied to be a teller at a bank and I've already had the interview but I go in for orientation next week on my days off."

"Wow this is happening fast." Allison lifted her finger.

"I know someone that cuts hair if you need a replacement for me right away."

"Oh, really." It wasn't a question. Lisa was almost gun shy.

"Yea. I can't say how her work ethic is, but she's licensed." At least Allison was honest.

At this point, Lisa was so tired that she didn't care if Allison worked for her or didn't. In fact, she didn't care much if the salon burned to the ground. It would be a hit to the wallet, but she was getting sick of everything. Her car had been vandalized, she had a gun toting Italian in her shop, and now her best stylist was leaving and recommending someone she didn't even know that well. It a terrible three days, and the next four proved to be worse.

CHAPTER 8:
A TALE OF TWO TOMMYS

Lisa was on the phone with the police for the third time in as many months when Anne came in with Ieva. She was a platinum blond like her brothers, and she was cute as a button. They sat in the lobby while Lisa held up her finger. There was no one else in the shop, and it had been a slow afternoon. Anne waved her off and handed Ieva her favorite tattered book that managed to keep her occupied no matter where they went. They waited patiently for her to get off the phone. Anne unabashedly eavesdropped on the call. Lisa was shaking her head.

"So there's nothing I can do? They can just put up cameras to spy on my customers and I can't do anything about it." She shook her head. She jabbed a finger at the button on the cordless phone and tossed it on the counter carelessly. "This is a load of crap. He needs to point his camera at his own salon and leave it there." Lisa whipped out the printed sheet for the chair and Ieva's eyes lit up when Lisa threw it over the barber seat. Lisa's troubles were suddenly gone.

"Wow!" she said, coming over to feel it with her fingers. Lisa didn't stop her and Anne gave her an imploring look. Lisa smiled.

"Would you like to have a haircut?" she asked the little girl. The little girl stopped in her tracks and she looked from her mother to the stylist and shook her head no. Lisa pulled out her CD player and put in a Disney CD. She tooled around the shop, bopping and dancing to the music. Ieva just laughed at her and inched closer to the chair. When Lisa stopped in front of it and patted it for her,

Ieva sat down in it. Lisa was winning. Anne pulled a large t-shirt out of her bag and handed it to Ieva. She put it on over her head and laughed when her arms got stuck inside. Thrusting them through the holes, she giggled harder and Lisa laughed with her. Anne looked at her.

"Straight across the forehead and then an inch or two off the back should do it." Lisa bobbed her head to the music and sang; Ieva was so busy singing along with her that she didn't realize that Lisa had started the haircut.

"You gotta be still, babe," Lisa told her. "You can have a sucker if you're super good." Candy was a good thing. Ieva looked shocked that someone would offer her a treat for being good and sat as still as stone for the rest of the haircut, still singing along to the songs. It was that simple, and soon, it was over. Lisa gave her two lollipops and she hopped down from the chair to show her mother the candy.

"Look Mama!!" she said proudly. Anne ruffled her freshly cut hair and Ieva sat down next to her. Lisa pulled the cover off the chair and invited Anne to sit. She shook her head.

"No, not me today, just her. How are things though?"

"Ok, I guess. Got some news the other day from my doctor..." Lisa trailed off with a smile. Anne looked at her with concern.

"Are you alright?"

"Yea, we're alright." Lisa smirked. She waited for Anne to catch up. Anne didn't.

"Did he say something was wrong?"

"No, he said we're both healthy."

"Did Larry go with you or something?" Larry was Lisa's husband, they had gotten married amid the insanity at the barber shop. Lisa broke into a huge grin and turned around to face Anne. Ieva was still eating her candy, flipping through her book.

"Nooooo," Lisa said to her. Lisa watched the wheels grinding in Anne's brain and then saw her mouth drop to her chin. It clicked.

"Lisa. LISA! Oh my god!" Anne squealed and Ieva dropped her book and squealed too. Lisa was pregnant! The two women hugged and Lisa started to tear up. Anne pulled a tissue out of a box on the counter.

"Oh my god, Lisa, congratulations!" Lisa beamed and Anne wiped Lisa's face.

"Don't you start that already!" Anne mopped her up and then put her hand on the top of Ieva's head, who hadn't stopped squealing yet. She stopped and picked up her book.

"Mom, go!" she exclaimed. Anne sighed.

"Well that's my cue," she said to Lisa. Lisa giggled. As Anne was leaving, Vincenzo was sweeping through the back door.

"Helloooo beautiful," he sang to her. Lisa smiled. Vincenzo was one of a kind, and she liked him, but she didn't want to tell him what she had to say. She took a deep breath.

"Vinny, we have to talk." She watched him nervously, wringing her hands. He grabbed them and held them still.

"What is it, *Bella*? Don't be so nervous."

"Well, I've hired a couple of new people and I'm moving you down to two days a week."

"Oh is that all?" He dropped her hands and waved her away. She was relieved that he hadn't lost his temper. "I knew that was coming."

"You did?"

"Sure, when Harry put his cameras in front of your door, I knew that my days were limited. Who did you hire?"

"Well, I hired a girl named Joan, and one of Allison's friends, Destiny. I also hired Tommy Ferrari, and I added a couple more days to Tommy the Marine's schedule." Damien had left Lisa after the incident with Raheleh, saying that he couldn't work in such a stressful environment. He was ready to start his own shop and hadn't mentioned where he might be going.

"What about Helga?" he asked her. Helga was a pinch hitter that Lisa sometimes called in when someone else called out. She and Tommy the Marine usually switched weekends regularly, so there was room for her on the schedule. The woman was nice enough, and was quiet and unassuming. She had been friends with Raheleh and still spoke to her, but Lisa wasn't sure how close they really were.

"I've added a couple of more days to her schedule too.

Everyone has about four shifts a week except for me, and you."
Vincenzo sighed.

"You discriminating against me," he said to her, pouting.

"Vinny, you have two jobs and a million dollars. You talk sly
to my clients. You annoy the other hairdressers. You brought a gun
into my shop and now the other salon owner that you work for is
stalking my door because he thinks that you're working for me,
which you are." That was all she said and he nodded. Vincenzo
shrugged.

"Well, at least you didn't fire me," he said, and walked around
to his station. Lisa just shook her head. He was incorrigible.

Joan came in that afternoon for her first shift. Joan was tall
and heavy set. She was good looking although her clothes were a
bit small; she dressed as if she had trouble finding clothes that
would fit her frame. She wasn't hugely overweight, she was
genuinely big boned. Joan came in with a caboodles box that had
some personal styling tools in it, and a lunch box that had her name
written in Sharpie on the outside.

"That's an awfully big box Joan, did you bring enough for me
too?" Lisa was joking although her curiosity was running rampant.

"As a matter of fact, if you're hungry I have extra." She
opened the box to show Lisa and it was full to the top with
Tupperware dishes and fresh fruit. Vincenzo sniffed.

"Why you carry around so much food?" he asked her. Lisa
noticed that he wasn't flirting. "I bet most of it came out of a can,"
he added. Joan ignored him.

"I have to carry around snacks and stuff because my blood
sugar gets low and I might pass out." Lisa had heard of this before.

"Oh yea," she said, shaking her finger. "What's that called
again? Hyper something?"

"Hypoglycemic," Joan filled in.

"Right!" Lisa exclaimed.

"Yes," said Joan. Vincenzo sniffed again but didn't speak. He
was quiet for the rest of his shift, which was rather unusual.

A few hours passed, and Joan looked antsy as they had
nothing to do. There were no customers in the shop and they were
standing around the chairs discussing everything under the sun.

Vincenzo was gone and the sun was on its way down. Joan picked up her cooler.

"Is it alright if I have a snack?" Joan asked.

"Yea," said Lisa, blithely. It's a medical thing, I get that. Eat whenever you want." Joan happily pulled out a sandwich with a bottle of water and demolished it. When two women walked in, they each took a seat while Lisa and Joan prepped the ladies for their services.

"These are some of my regular clients, Tiffany and Brenda Nicely. We'll give them a haircut and then you prep one to highlight while I fix the other lady first and then I'll come and do highlights on her. Joan talked to Lisa while they were working.

"Who am I going to work with tomorrow?" Joan asked her. Lisa mentally looked at the schedule, tilting her head.

"I think you're with Tommy Linguini and Helga tomorrow. They usually work a weekend, but I've got an appointment to keep myself so I called them both in since its Tommy's day off.

"Ok, today is Tommy's day off, but Tommy also works? Is there more than one?" Joan looked confused. Lisa nodded.

"As a matter of fact, there are," she told Joan. "There's Tommy Linguini also known as Tommy the Marine. He's an old military barber that used to have a shop in New Canaan called the Marine Barber shop. He's going to be working with you tomorrow. Then you've got Fast Talking Thomas Ferrari, who usually goes by Tommy, but here we call him Ferrari because we already have a Tommy."

"Sounds confusing."

"Only on Thursday when I do the schedule, but you'll get used to it. Just remember Tommy the Marine and Fast Ferrari. You'll know the difference really soon, I promise." Joan smiled and toweled off her customer's hair. Lisa was already cutting and had a box pulled out with powdered highlight bleach waiting for her on the counter.

"Who else works here?" Joan asked.

"Well, there's you Joan, and me. Vinny is the Italian guy you met this afternoon, and there's another woman, Helga. Destiny is a young girl that comes in and does a lot of color jobs for me and a few haircuts." The customer in Lisa's chair snorted and shook her head minutely. Lisa leaned down and looked at her.

"What's up?" Lisa asked. The ladies in the chair were Brenda and Tiffany – they came in on the same day every week to get their hair cut and once a month they got the works: a shampoo, a haircut, and highlights put in. The ladies were in their mid-thirties and had been some of Lisa's first customers in the new salon and had probably seen as much in the salon as Anne had. As they got to know Lisa, they stopped coming in and stuck to Lisa. No one else could color them like she could, they had told her. Tiffany, the younger woman now getting a trim from Joan, spoke first.

"That girl that you're talking about Destiny is trying to undercut your clientele." Tiffany didn't cut words, and that was a pretty heavy accusation. This was a business where you got paid by the ticket. In the world of hair, people were extremely picky. Loyalty was everything with your hairdresser. If you were kind to them, they took care of you, and your hair, and sometimes, things blossomed in a salon without any prompting. Brenda nodded.

"Yea, Lisa, last time Tiff and I were here, Destiny did Tiffany's hair. She told me and Tiff that we needed to wait to get our highlights put in until she was there to do them for you. She bragged that her cuts were better. All kinds of sarcastic back biting crap." Lisa shook her head.

"It'll be alright." Lisa knew better than to blow up at salon gossip, so she didn't dwell on the idea. She wondered nostalgically about Orv and how he was doing in his shop across the way. Brenda just shrugged. Joan had Tiffany prepped and was getting ready to trade places with Lisa so that Lisa could put highlights in. Brenda had short hair, and she was already in the waiting phase.

"Anyone else?" Joan asked.

"No, I'm pretty sure that's it." Joan walked over to her cooler and pulled out an apple. Tiffany looked at her strangely and then exchanged a glance with Brenda. The pair didn't say anything, but Lisa smiled knowing that the situation would be discussed between the two of them. Lisa moved over to Tiff's chair. Working quickly, she put in the foil and then went back to Brenda. It was getting late, and Lisa lost herself to the job as the sun went down on her little shop.

The next day, Joan was set to work with Tommy the Marine. He did an ok job; he served a small niche cutting giving military style haircuts. He was a bit stern, but he was fun. Tommy had lots of stories and served in more than one war; telling the story of his anchor tattoo was the highlight of most days for him. He would wax on about the war and cut hair. Tommy was a decent barber. Joan and Tommy cut hair well together, and it wasn't long before Helga came in behind the two of them and took up her chair.

Helga was tall, with high cheekbones, and light brown hair. She was kind of quiet and when she spoke she had a slight accent. Joan found out that she was from Estonia, and when she had a notion to talk to someone, she would talk about her home country. Helga was in idle conversation with Joan when Tommy the Marine walked by and pinched her on the butt. She laughed and waved him away.

"Not at work," she laughed. Joan's brow furrowed, and Tommy must have seen it. He turned to her and lifted his hands up to Joan's chest level.

"Jealous, honey?" he asked her, pretending to squeeze her. He hadn't touched her, but she moved away anyhow.

"Definitely not," Joan told him. She had just had a customer sit down in her chair, luckily that hadn't seen the interaction. The customer was waiting patiently, but Joan had disappeared into the back room. Tommy went to investigate.

"What are you doing?" he asked her bluntly. She was eating. "You can't take a break now; you have a client in the chair."

"I have a medical problem, I need to eat."

"Well, come on out here when you're done." Tommy looked perturbed. "This isn't a restaurant, you know." Helga leaned over and peered into the back room while this was going on. She was giving a woman a layered look and was almost finished.

"I'll do it," Helga said thickly. "You want me to finish it? I will," she offered, "but I get to keep the ticket."

"That's a good girl," the old marine said to Helga. Helga smiled and turned her shoulders flirtatiously. Joan finished her snack and walked out of the back room; she approached her client that had waited for his haircut and leaned down to him.

"Like I said, I have a medical condition where if I don't eat regularly, I could get the shakes, pass out, or if I leave it long enough, go into a coma. I apologize." She said it loudly enough for everyone to hear. The customer smiled and shook his head.

"It's fine," he said. "She explained what she was doing before she left me sitting here." He directed this to Tommy and Helga. Tommy just shrugged.

"Well, if it's all the same to you then," was all he replied. It wasn't as pleasant as it had been in the morning time. Tommy continued to bump Helga frequently, and patted her on the ass whenever he felt the need to congratulate her. Joan on the other hand, was a bit sullen. It was fine. Lisa didn't hear about it until the next week, when Joan recounted the situation to her while they had a shift together. Lisa had inquired when she noticed Joan hadn't had anything to eat in a few hours. She was becoming sluggish and sleepy during her last cut.

"Why don't you go for lunch and then come back and rest. I'll give you the hour off. Vincenzo should be here for his shift soon, so there would be two of us." Joan liked the sound of it and took off. She hurried back and was in the shop eating lunch before Vincenzo could even arrive at the back door. By the time he did, she was laying on the couch, dozing. Vincenzo sneered in her direction.

"What kind of place are you running here? Is this for kindergarteners?" Lisa glared at Vincenzo's lip.

"I decide who does what around here," she snapped at him, ruffled. For whatever reason, he didn't like Joan, and that was fine with Lisa, but she expected them to act professional. She didn't want another episode of "Percy is looking at Damien." Of course, professional might be a little difficult with Joan on snoring loudly on the comfortable couch that served as a place for clients to sit. Lisa was still dizzy from wondering what to do about Tommy the Marine.

"Furthermore," she added, "You're on your last leg already, watch your mouth." That was all she said and she turned on her heel to stomp to her office. When she shut the door behind her,

Vincenzo sauntered up to the couch and shook Joan roughly.

"Naptime's over sweetheart." She sat up and stretched. Vincenzo and Joan worked together for the rest of the afternoon. He was solid and quiet. Finally, when the shop was empty, he rapped on Lisa's door then let himself in and shut the door behind her.

"Do something about that behemoth out there," he fired at her without preamble.

"Huh?" Lisa looked up at him. She had been day dreaming of painting a nursery with her paperwork in front of her for the last hour.

"She doesn't even fit her clothes!" he was trying to whisper but it was coming out angrily. Lisa tried to think of what Joan had been wearing. A skirt?

"Her blouse is so low that the tops are falling out, and she's got this skirt on that looks like it wants to give up and be a curtain. Please!" Vincenzo looked so serious that she couldn't help but laugh.

"I'm serious *Bella,* please, she is bad for business!!" Lisa looked at him thoughtfully. She tilted her head to the side.

"Vinny?" she said questioningly.

"Yes?"

"You're fired." He didn't argue.

"Fine!" he said, throwing up his hands. "Why, *Bella*?" She just shook her head. Vincenzo left her office and gathered up his things without a word to anyone. Lisa waited until she heard the back door sweep open and slam shut again. It rattled the back wall, but otherwise, as quickly as he had come, he was gone. She sighed and rubbed her belly.

Lisa called Destiny and asked her to cover the rest of the shift, and when she arrived, Lisa left the shop with the schedule under her arm. Taking a last glance, she knew that she had made the right decision in firing Vincenzo. Joan was wearing a knee length skirt and a nice top, though perhaps a bit low cut for her. It wasn't bad.

As she got into her car at the garage, she saw Anne pull in across the street at her shop. She almost wished she hadn't left as early as she had, but Lisa was just too exhausted. Pulling away, she headed home.

Anne however, was not to be deterred. It was time for a color job and a good haircut. She was alone this time, and had a couple of free hours. She was ready to listen to Lisa's stories and gossip. When she came in, Destiny and Joan were sweeping up and there was a client in Joan's chair getting ready to pull off his smock and leave. Destiny waved her over to the chair and sat her down.

"Hi, I'm Destiny, and I'll be your stylist today." She folded her hands together in mock seriousness and stood in front of her. Anne wanted to wrinkle her nose at Destiny's outfit. Destiny was short and a bit overweight for her frame, but not too much. Her choice in clothing was not as tasteful; she was wearing low rider jeans and a midriff top, but her body was spilling out of the bottom of the shirt and hanging over the top of her pants. The top was too tight for her ample bosom and the spaghetti straps were hanging on for dear life over her shoulders. She looked a bit sloppy but Anne would never ever tell her that. She smiled instead.

"Where's Lisa?" Anne asked, looking around. Destiny crinkled her nose.

"Vinny got fired today and she went home just a little bit ago."

"Aw," Anne said, "I wanted to get my hair colored while I was here." Destiny walked over and patted the chair.

"I can color it for you," she replied. "I can do a better job than Lisa too, I bet." Joan looked over at Destiny out of the corner of her eye and raised an eyebrow but didn't say a word. Anne shook her head.

"No, not this time, I think." She sat down in Destiny's chair. "I think I'll just get a wash and a trim if you don't mind."

"Oh, come on, I do great color. I see that you've got some darker roots showing right here. The blond looks like it's starting to turn brassy at the bottom too." Anne's secret was even though her children had platinum blond hair, her natural color was a mousy brown. Her blonde children had everything to do with Arnie. Destiny continued outing her.

"You could go a bit darker on the blonde and add some sunny highlights. It'll be better than anything Lisa ever did." Anne sighed. She didn't have anything else to do, and she did like the idea Destiny was presenting.

"Alright then," she capitulated. Destiny cranked the chair up and got to work. The call Lisa would get from Anne later would infuriate her. Destiny did not do as she had said she would – she dyed Anne's hair a dark brown instead of a blonde and then had put bleachy highlights in.

"It's not going to be this dark when I'm finished," Destiny had promised. Anne went home that day in tears of fury. Lisa made an appointment with her for the next week and would fix Anne's hair for free. Loyalty was everything. Destiny, having only been there six short months was going to be out the door if she wasn't careful. What other kinds of mishaps had there been? Lisa didn't have time for mistakes to walk out of her salon doors. Joan would recount the situation to her with sympathy for Anne and a benefit of the doubt tone for Destiny. Tommy the Marine was not so sympathetic towards Destiny, and he told her so one afternoon some days later.

Joan and Lisa were cleaning up and getting ready to leave; Tommy was getting ready to start his shift, and Ferrari was due in any second.

"You need to go ahead and fire her," Tommy said to Lisa as she wiped the countertop behind her. "She's screwing you up," he said to her, shaking a wrinkled finger in her direction. Lisa didn't reply; she just kept wiping. He harrumphed and didn't have time to say anything before Ferrari swung the door open and stumped in.

Ferrari was short and stocky with a big barrel chest; but most people were more curious about his pronounced limp. To look at him, you could quite possibly guess his name – he even looked like someone you'd call Ferrari. The man talked quickly with a nasally Yankee accent and didn't mince words. The chronic New Yorker had been a dock hand for many years and was quite weathered. He had an old fashioned pompadour with sideburns and was fond of wearing white t-shirts and jeans like James Dean. At the interview when Lisa had asked him why he wanted to work in a salon, he had pulled a comb out and ran it around the side of his head and shrugged.

"What can I say, I've always loved cutting hair," he'd replied.

"So, I got my barbering license a long time ago." Lisa couldn't argue with that and hired him on the spot. When he came into the shop that day, his bad leg must have been acting up because he had brought his cane and was leaning heavily onto it.

"Hey you guys, what's happening?" He wasted no time getting his booth organized and ready for himself. Joan gave him a friendly little wave and packed her cooler. Lisa put down the broom.

"You ok today, Ferrari," she asked him.

"Yea, I left the air conditioner on in my apartment and this bum leg stiffened up last night. Can't get it to wake up right." He shook his head and shrugged.

"How'd you get that limp anyway?" Tommy asked curiously.

"Got shot. Messed me up." The Marine straightened up.

"Did you serve in the war?" Ferrari shook his head.

"My third wife's ex-husband shot me right in the ass for sleeping with his wife. Right. In. The. Ass."

"He was aiming for it?" Ferrari shrugged.

"Eh, it was in the air."

Tommy the Marine burst into laughter while Joan and Lisa nearly collapsed on each other with giggles. Ferrari looked around confused.

"What?!" he asked them. None of them could say a word.

CHAPTER 9:
HAIR HERE, AND ABROAD

The times of laughter in the shop continued as the clients swung in and out. Things were going well at the shop and Lisa was getting big. Her feet were starting to swell and her tummy was rounding out nicely. She was only weeks away. As a result, things had been hectic around the shop. Lisa was in the shop less and less – her doctor had put her on bed rest, but Lisa hadn't been listening to her doctor, she had been working as all hard working women tend to do. At least she was lucky enough to have a few decent employees and a couple of regulars that kept her spirits up.

She still had Ferrari and Tommy the Marine, both of whom were dependable enough to get things done. There was still Destiny, who was getting more and more complaints. Lisa was going to have to face the fact that Destiny really was trying to take her clients from underneath her, but Lisa still couldn't afford to fire her. Helga was working part time; Joan had been there for four months, and was speaking to Lisa about quitting when she asked if Joan could take another day.

"I can't," she said to Lisa. "I'm getting to where I can't stand on my feet all day like that...in fact, I was thinking about putting in my two weeks." Joan pulled out a piece of paper from her

cooler. It had been rolled up and was a bit damp. She handed it to Lisa.

"Are you serious?" Lisa was close to whining. Joan nodded slowly.

"It's not anything here," Joan said to Lisa. "It's my health. My hypoglycemia is one thing, but my feet and stuff are starting to swell when I work the long days." Lisa could sure talk about some feet swelling, she thought as she looked at her own puffy ankles.

"Well, what are you going to do next?"

"I was thinking flowers."

"Flowers?"

"Yea, I thought that I would try my hand at making floral arrangements. Haven't you ever seen big Valentine's arrangements? I love those! It's something that I like to do, and I'm very good at it, or so I like to think." Lisa smiled at Joan.

"Well, I wish you the best," she said to her. She didn't feel the smile on her face, but she kept it there. She rubbed her big belly. Destiny would be there this afternoon and she was getting ready to leave. Just then, Tommy the Marine came out of the rest room, drying his hands on a paper towel.

"I know someone that cuts hair too," he said to Lisa. "If you want I can give her a call." Lisa smiled, and sighed with relief. Cute foreign gal with a nice husband and a coupla kids.

"Thank you, Tommy, that would be wonderful." He nodded and that was that. She left the shop in their hands, taking home with her a stack of applications. When she was on the floor the next day, Anne came in with Erik, who was nearly up to Lisa's hip already. Time was really flying; Lisa hadn't seen Erik in a while – he who was a bouncing baby was now a precocious four year old with shockingly blonde hair. It was that moment when she realized that she had worked in her own shop for almost five years.

"Anne, I can't believe how big he's gotten!" Lisa exclaimed. Erik stood there in the barber shop and just observed for a moment. He was like that, Lisa had noticed: quiet and observant while not entirely shy. Joan, who loved kids, dragged out the cartoon covered smock and held it up for him.

"Can I cut your hair?" she asked him. He shook his head and

sat down in the waiting area, shouldering a superhero backpack and pulling out his distractions. She put away the smock and took the broom from the back room. Anne sat in Lisa's chair and spun around in it for good measure, until she was facing the mirror.

"Can I watch?" she asked Lisa.

"Sure, I can wet you down with a spray bottle," she told Anne, grabbing the small spritzer that hung on a hook in her station. Soon, Lisa was snipping away and chatting off-handedly.

"Hey, Lisa did you know that Damien has his own barber shop now?" Anne asked her.

"No kidding?!" she said. "I wonder if he's put foil on the windows to keep people from stealing his haircuts, yet."

"I don't think you can steal a crew cut and besides, you'd have to scale the building to peep in the windows.

"Yea, you know where that shoe place is down town that does all of the specialty repairs and stuff? There's a room for rent upstairs in the same building there and Damien's got it. He's cutting men's hair. Arnie looked him up and found him after he left your place," she told Lisa. "He said that Damien doesn't even have any running water or anything at all."

"I'm no lawyer, but isn't that against the law?" asked Lisa. Hairdressing and barbering professions had strict hygiene standards and she was pretty sure that was a huge health violation. It wouldn't be long before the health department took his credentials if he continued.

"I don't know, you tell me; you're the hairdresser." That she was. And Lisa was true to her word too – she cut and fixed the color in Anne's hair for free when Destiny messed it up, and made up for any of the other mistakes that were made. Lisa shrugged and silently hoped that his business did well enough so that he would stay out of her hair. Anne continued.

"Anyway, that's not all," she said with a twinkle in her eye. Lisa's eyebrow shot up. What else? "Arnie said the whole place stinks like shoe polish and that Damien is giving free horoscope readings with his haircuts." Lisa had to laugh out loud, her rounded tummy jogging with the effort. Joan looked up from her sweeping.

"Weird!" she said to the pair of them. "Who does that?"

86

"Damien," Lisa and Anne said together, and then laughed.

"He's a barber that used to work for me, Joan; Anne's husband Arnie used to come in all the time and get his haircut." Lisa fluffed Anne's hair.

"Where is Arnie these days?" she asked the woman in the chair.

"Daddy works a lot," piped Erik. He was so quiet that Lisa had forgotten that he was in there. Anne's eyes met with Lisa's in the mirror and she shook her head minutely. Lisa frowned at her and tried to apologize with her eyes. Instead she swung Anne around so that they could see the little boy and wouldn't forget their tongues anymore. Joan, who had immediately picked up the vibration in the air, pulled out her snack cooler with a loud scrape along the floor and held it up.

"Anyone hungry? I brought a lot of good stuff today." Lisa's belly rumbled and her bladder felt urgent. She ignored the latter and raised her hand. Erik was interested too, and looked at Anne for a cue.

"Erik, she's offering, would you like something?" Erik nodded and picked a fruit cup out of Joan's lunch pail. She dug around inside and pulled out a small container of hot wings. Lisa lit up.

"Ahh!" she said to Joan. Joan nodded. "I brought these just for you girl, with extra hot sauce and ranch." Lisa's mouth watered. Her pregnant body had consumed some strange things and more often than not in the last four months, she had hit Joan up for something to eat. Joan pulled out some peanut butter crackers and milk for herself. Lisa kept cutting and Anne steered the conversation out of dangerous waters.

"So, have you found anyone to replace Vinny?" she asked. Lisa nodded.

"I found a couple of good candidates, and I'm doing some interviews this week. I think I'll hire two people since *someone*," she said pointedly in Joan's direction, "wants to turn in a two weeks' notice and become a florist." Joan laughed at her.

"I can't help it," she said to Lisa, laughing. Lisa smiled at her and put her scissors down on the counter. Brushing Anne's shoulders off, Lisa spritzed her hair again and began styling it.

"I know," she said, "but I'm going to miss you."

"Your pregnant butt is going to miss my cooler." Anne and Lisa both laughed out loud at this. They were still laughing when Anne left the salon with Erik politely in tow. As she opened the door to the salon, a striking Asian woman with a severe posture hustled in. She held the door for Anne to leave and then addressed Lisa with clipped and proper English.

"You're Lisa?" the newcomer asked her. Lisa smiled and put her hand out.

"Yes, you must be Huong," Lisa said. Tommy the Marine had instructed her to talk to Lisa about getting a job. She had already fired Vincenzo and now Joan was leaving too. He had said that Huong was a "boat person" - meaning a refugee from war era Vietnam. However long she had been here, she was Westernized and fitting in to say the least. Huong was willowy and tall but curvy, and her hair was braided and wrapped around her head so that it would not touch the ground. Lisa could tell that it was very long. Joan smiled at her, and as another client came in, Lisa looked around at her.

"Joan, take this one and I'm going to give her an interview then take off for a while. My back is killing me." Lisa motioned towards her office and Joan nodded; she sat the customer down and they began to chat while Huong followed Lisa into her office and sat down. Huong folded her hands in her lap and waited patiently for Lisa to start. When she sat behind her desk, Lisa pulled out the application that people normally started with and clipped it to a board and handed it to Huong.

"You can fill this out while we talk." As Huong took the application and began to scribble on it, Lisa asked:

"So, how long have you been cutting hair?"

"Well, I came to United States in 1979, after the end of the war. I was 11. "I lived with my older sister above a barber shop in New York. We had been begging in the streets but the woman in the barber shop noticed us and started making us sandwiches. Her husband, who managed the shop, would let my sister sweep the floors. When I was old enough to start sweeping he put me to work and my sister ran away to get married. That's how I met Captain

Linguini, he came into the shop and right away knew we were Vietnamese. I fell in love with the smells and sounds of the shop. I eventually went to school to get my license." Huong pulled out a small card and a set of papers from her handbag and handed them to Lisa. Sure enough, she was licensed, and had recently been recertified.

"Looks good to me," said Lisa. "I have a full time position open now, and one that will be available in two weeks. Is that ok?" Lisa was ready to hire her. Turning around with the documents in her hand she made a copy with the machine the tiny table behind the desk. She wasn't *desperate* per se, but she was looking to fill in the schedule with people that she could depend on. The weeks to her due date were counting down very quickly, and she was still supposed to be on bed rest. Huong would be a great addition to the team, she could tell. However, Huong looked disappointedly back at Lisa from the other side of the desk.

"Miss Lisa," she began. "I have four small children and a husband that works long hours. Could I please just have part time?" Huong looked worried and Lisa could sympathize. What she couldn't do, if she intended to hire Huong was argue.

"Well, I really need a stylist that can work full time, but I need someone now, so I suppose that you'll get your part time."

"Thank you, my husband leaves very early in the morning and comes home in the middle of the afternoon about three. I can work any time after that. We do need the money." That was perfect; she needed someone for the afternoon.

"I like the way that sounds," agreed Lisa. Huong put a finger to the side of her chin and looked away for a moment.

"I know something else that might help us, too," she told her new boss. "I have a friend here that was also a refugee in Vietnam. She is older than me, but what we have in common most is a love of hair. She styled hair for a matchmaker for many years back home. She helps me braid mine sometimes, and she went to school in Connecticut to be a stylist. She lives in Danbury now but she would come and cut hair for you part time to make up for my hours." Lisa nodded thoughtfully.

"Danbury?" Lisa asked. That was almost an hour away.

"Yes, she says she wants to come to New Canaan to work so that she can rub kneecaps with rich people."

"Kneecaps?" Huong shrugged.

"Elbows," said Lisa. "I'll take her number; I still have some interviews to complete but I can't make any promises. In the meantime you can come in tomorrow at 4, that should give your husband plenty of time to get home and then I'll put you on the schedule this Thursday for all next week." Lisa stood up and stuck her hand out again. Huong took it firmly and thanked her, bowing out of the office. When she turned, she was met with a familiar face.

"Captain Linguini!" she said, hugging him tight. He was much older than her, Lisa could tell, but there was affection, none the less. Tommy the Marine did not try and flirt with her; he simply put his arms around her shoulders and turned her towards Lisa. She could see them both smiling from ear to ear, what might have been a proud father and his daughter for a visit.

"You're going to love her," he beamed at Lisa. She hoped he was right. Tommy and Huong made small talk while Lisa got her things together. Waving at everyone and nodding at Joan who still had three more hours left on her shift, she left the shop, happy at least that she had done something productive. She would make a couple of more calls that night and rearrange the schedule at home.

Tommy the Marine and Joan were alone in the shop for a while. Ferrari would be in to relieve Joan in just a little bit, but Joan's energy was flagging. She yawned and yawned until Tommy the Marine finally told her, "Hey, go on over there and take a nap if you're so tired." Joan obliged – it didn't take much, and soon it was Tommy the Marine and a blissfully snoring Joan on the couch.

Lisa went home that afternoon and flipped through the applications that she had taken home the other day. Here was Shannon, who formerly worked for Shear Madness. There was Alejandra, who had worked at the salon that Ashley had started in, The Yankee Clipper Barbershop. They were both good candidates, and in matter of moments, she had made the calls that would bring them in for interviews. That night, she and Larry slept soundly with the hope of a new day, the baby squirming in her belly as she lay drifting away.

The next morning, Lisa didn't feel well so she called Ferrari to take her shift while she rested. He wouldn't like the Wednesday morning shift – it was too slow for him and he would end up pacing back and forth. Destiny would be there to help him, and there would be a bit of time that there was nothing that they could do except entertain each other. He had complained before that there wasn't enough clients to keep himself busy and often found himself bouncing around the salon like a ping pong ball. Shortly after Lisa got back home and was relaxing on the couch, the phone rang. It was Ferrari.

"Yea, are you there?" he said to her. He sounded worried ; at least, he was talking so fast that Lisa could hardly understand him.

"Yea it's me," she said into the phone. "What's up?"

"I'm in the stock room right now; I was thinking maybe you should hear this." Lisa was confused but could hear Ferrari fumbling with the door knob to the back room. When it opened, she could hear Destiny bragging in the background.

"Yea, she's good and all, but she doesn't know how to run this place. She's got this old ass ticket system straight out of some barber shop from the 40's." Pause. "No, she's not as good as me, I'm better." Pause. "Sometimes, but I don't really know when she's going to be around, and besides, I've got more skills in my little finger than she has in her whole pregnant body." Ferrari put the phone up to his ear.

"You hear that?" he said.

"Yea," said Lisa flatly.

"She's on the business phone with one of your clients."

"You're kidding, right? How do you know?"

"She took the client list out of the log book when she thought I wasn't looking and she's been making phone calls since." Lisa's eyes bugged out of her head on her end of the phone but she couldn't speak.

"What do you want me to do?" asked Ferrari. Lisa considered it.

"Let her finish what she's doing and act like nothing ever happened." Ferrari sniffed.

"Alright, I guess," he said to her. Tears of fury in her eyes, she punched the button on the phone. Picking up the stack of applications, she thumbed through them again before she left the house and picked out two more to call while she was at the shop. On the way in, she called Helga and asked her to meet at the salon. Helga would be waiting. What she saw was typical in any salon, but what lay underneath pumped poison into Lisa's thoughts.

In the time it took for Lisa to gather herself and arrive, Destiny had cut a woman's hair and was telling her that she needed some layers. Lisa saw Destiny for the first time that day. The ill-fitting clothes and the bright make up. Lisa saw the "better than everyone attitude" in action. Destiny was leaning over the customer with her hand on the woman's shoulder. Lisa recognized it as a sales tactic more than an affectionate gesture. Her posture was sloppy and she snapped her gum while she talked.

"Hey Destiny," Lisa said to her. Destiny straightened up. "Are you finished with that client." It wasn't a question. The client looked at Lisa gratefully and leaned forward.

"Yes", said the pretty brunette in the chair. "I've been done for a few minutes now." The woman shook the hair off her herself in the smock and took it off, handing it to Destiny. She handed Lisa the money to pay for the haircut and walked out without neither a compliment nor a complaint, only a word of thanks. Lisa turned her attention to Destiny and affixed what she hoped was a laser like stare. Destiny looked back at her.

"What?" she asked sarcastically. She wasn't expecting Lisa and looked like a deer in the headlights. Her bravado came across as sulking.

"Let me tell you something about my 'skills' chick. This is *my* shop. This is my job, my business. If you can do it better, you go start your own shop. If you want to badmouth me, you can prove how good you are somewhere else." Lisa only had a couple of sentences left before she would run out of simple and nice things to say. She let silence fall.

"I never said that I was better than you, Lisa, I would never say that." Strike one. Lisa sniffed.

"Just exactly what makes you think you can do better than me running this business?"

"Well, I mean…I don't have a problem with the way you do things Lisa; I have a few suggestions that might help, but otherwise, it's your business. I would never say anything about you like that." Strike two.

"What are you doing on the phone with my clients?"

"I've never called any of your clients." Strike three. Lisa picked up the log book from its spot on the counter and threw it across the room. It landed on the couch that was there for customers in a heap of papers and loose sheets that fell to the floor and spread about.

"Where's my client list?!" she shouted. She crossed the distance to Destiny's cubby hole and raked her hand along the supplies that were in there, knocking them to the ground. Ferrari and Destiny both spoke at the same time.

"I don't have it!"

"She stuffed it in her pocket." Lisa looked at Ferrari. He nodded almost imperceptibly. She turned back to Destiny.

"Give it up," she said to Destiny, holding out her hand. Destiny shook her head. Lisa closed the distance, her pregnant belly between them. "Give it to me," she repeated. Destiny reached a shaking hand in her pocket and pulled out the list. Lisa snatched it from her hand and stepped back, pointing at the door.

"Now get out." Destiny sulkily picked up her purse and left the supplies on the floor. She flounced out and the bell tinkled behind her as she went.

"Lisa, you ok?" Ferrari asked her. She felt a sharp pain her abdomen, but nodded anyway.

"Ferrari, Helga is coming in to cover the rest of Destiny's shift, and Joan will be in to relieve you. Tommy is coming in to overlap for the post lunch crowd and I'll be here all afternoon doing interviews. Do you think you could cover it until then?" Ferrari nodded and stumped away. Lisa interviewed four people that day; Alejandra, who turned out to be a beautiful Columbian woman with long curly hair, and Shannon, who still worked for the competition. She had called Huong's friend and penciled her in. In a burst of inspiration, she called a temp service to interview two

93

receptionists, and hired one on the spot. She figured at least if they didn't cut hair they had no reason to steal her clients. Lisa told them all to come in at the same time and told the rest of her employees that they needed to be here at the shop at 9pm Friday for a meeting.

When she drove home later that evening after closing up the shop, she felt her first pangs of false labor. They would last on and off for weeks, but Lisa had no idea.

CHAPTER 10:
FOR THE LOVE OF HAIR

Friday had rolled around and the group sat there in the salon. Ferrari and Tommy the Marine had Helga sandwiched on the couch that was reserved for customers. Ferrari was inching a little farther away from Tommy and Helga while they flirted; occasionally, Tommy would reach over and put his hand on Helga's knee. Huong and Hue, the new part timers sat together in front of the window at a table and chairs, chatting quietly in Vietnamese. Shannon and Joan sat in the salon chairs and Alejandra was standing behind Joan, talking to her about hair and fluffing out Joan's tresses while Shannon powdered her nose and commented from time to time. Stacie sat behind a newly installed podium style desk in an office chair. It held a phone for her to answer and the log book for haircuts, client lists and appointments.

A pizza delivery man stepped in front of the door and waved. Lisa let him in and pulled out her order – enough for everyone to have some – paid him, and as people grabbed the steaming slices, she started her meeting. Everyone had been introduced so she just got down to business.

"Ok, so there are some new rules. Number one, no more personal calls on the salon telephone unless it's an emergency. Stacie here," she said, gesturing to the older woman at the podium, who waved, "Is here to answer the phone and take their appointments. She's to ask who the client wants the appointment with and then she's going to schedule them according to your schedule. If they don't know, they just come in." Helga sniffed and shook her head, but said nothing.

"Second, you all need to put your tickets in the locked box underneath the podium when you're finished with them. The tickets are going to have numbers on them so if there are any missing, we'll know about it, because the tickets numbers will match to the log book. Any questions, so far?" Helga shook her head.

"I don't understand exactly why we should have to make appointments through someone else, now." Lisa pointed at her. Helga, who Lisa knew wasn't taking anything, didn't understand – she had a few loyal clients herself that called her to make an appointment. The thing was, if Lisa didn't put her foot down, what would happen next?

"Because I don't want people thinking that they can walk in here and use my facilities for free while I pay for all of the supplies along with what they get on commission. I'm over being stolen from and I'm over being lied to. Is there something wrong with that?" Helga's lips tightened but she said nothing in return. Ferrari turned in his seat.

"Do you think there's going to be more business? Why did you hire so many new people?" Ferrari didn't think the salon was busy enough as it is, so he had good reason to ask.

"Ferrari, I hired Stacie to take the books because of the pranks that Destiny pulled. Joan is going in two weeks, and so I hired two people to replace her that each work part time. Shannon is here to replace Destiny."

"I could have used more hours," spoke Helga again. She was looking more agitated than ever and was starting to get haughty. Lisa nodded and rubbed her belly.

"Don't worry, you'll have them. I'm about to be out of the salon most of the time, and I'm going to need you guys. Anything else?" Everyone shook their heads. "Alright, feel free to do what you like then, we're done." The groups broke up and Lisa went into the stock room to put some things away. She heard Helga talking to Tommy the Marine and the others.

"She is so grouchy, she needs a good screwing." Lisa dropped the box she was holding and was struggling to bend over and get it as the conversation continued. She had heard Joan gasp and Tommy the Marine guffaw.

"You all think I am kidding, but no! She needs a good screwing, it always sets things right with a grouchy woman."

"Does your husband feel that way?" asked Tommy the Marine playfully.

"My husband lets me do whatever I want. And I let him do whatever he wants. Sometimes we find other couples and swap."

"Oh wow", said Joan softly. "I'm out of here." Lisa heard her jump out of the chair and Ferrari yawn.

"Yea, I'm out of here too," he claimed. One by one they filed out and it was Stacie that finally left Lisa alone in the store room. Lisa was still stunned by the admissions that Helga had made, and wanted to giggle at her accusations that sex could solve all of her problems. Rubbing her belly, Lisa rather thought that sex was perhaps instead the root of her problem. It just further proved that it's always the quiet ones and no matter how much you thought you knew someone, they could always surprise you. Lisa went home that night and stayed in bed for the weekend while the shop took care of itself without her. It was good practice for when Joey came.

And from the looks of it, it would be fine. Joan's last day was the upcoming Saturday, and Huong and her friend that she'd gotten hired Hue were loyal employees and excellent hairdressers. They were both kind to the clients, and patiently listened when the clients didn't know what they wanted. When the two of them worked together, they talked about Vietnam. Tommy the Marine was on shift with them when stories started getting passed around.

"How'd you get over here, Hue?" asked Tommy?

"I left Vietnam on a boat that got captured by pirates." Tommy the Marine didn't bat an eyelash – there were plenty of people looking to steal and kill refugees in those days. Hue continued. "The pirates were bad men; they killed all the men in the boat and took the women and children hostage. I got sold to two VC's and they took me to a rich house with other girls. They tried to make me a hooker but the place got all shot up so I ran. I got on another boat and we were picked up at sea by soldiers."

"So, you didn't have no papers," said the old Marine, nodding. "How old are ya?"

"I'm 35," Hue said boldly. Huong snorted. *She* was 35 and she knew that Hue was older than she was. Tommy the Marine picked right up on it.

"If you're 35, I'm 50!" he chortled at her. Hue looked affronted and began to speak rapidly, her English breaking up and mixing with her native tongue.

"Don't you know it's rude to ask lady how old she is? My lawyer husband thinks I'm 24!"

"You told Lisa you were 23," said Huong smugly. Hue glared at her.

"You mind your business!" Hue told her. "I don't know how old I am, I can't remember back that far!

"Where's your papers?" asked the marine again. Hue looked a little sad.

"I lost my birth certificate on the way over and you Americans didn't know your numbers!"

Tommy broke up at that and was still laughing about when Alejandra came in to relieve him. As Tommy swept the floor and recounted the story, Alejandra came to Hue's defense.

"You don't ask a lady how old she is, and she has a right to lie. It's no one's business." Alejandra smiled and Tommy just shook his head.

"*Women,*" was all he could reply. He would tell that story for the next few days to anyone that would listen, but never when Hue was around. Joan gave him an obligatory chuckle and ignored him for the rest of the time. When there was a lull in the clients, she laid down on the couch for her usual afternoon siesta. Tommy did not complain, and no longer woke her when clients started to come in. Since he was to stuff the tickets in the box to be counted at the end of the day by Lisa, he had given away less and less haircuts to anyone that didn't want to work. While Joan slept, a regular client that Lisa had known for some time came in and sat in Tommy's chair.

"Hi there, beautiful," he said. "Tommy Linguini, at your service." He kissed her hand and his lips trailed up her wrist.

98

Yanking her hand away, the lady looked at him and laughed nervously.

"I'm nearly 70," she said to him, trying to discourage him.

"Well that's alright, I'm 86 next month. I like my women a little spry. What's your name, honey?"

"Emma Demato. My husband is Victor." Emma tensed while Tommy rested his hands on her shoulders.

"Can I cut your hair?" he asked her delicately. His hands began to move along her neck, and then down her shoulders to the hem of her shirt. She tried to pull away from him and he held her there for a moment, his hands sliding down her chest and into her shirt towards her breasts. She jumped up from the chair, flushing.

"No, I don't think so; I'll come when Lisa is here." The old woman left the salon in a hurry, and the call that Lisa got that night at home from Victor was a flaming mess. He wanted to threaten Tommy, and wanted Lisa to fire him. Lisa couldn't help but agree, but she wanted to hear Tommy's story first. Lisa believed Victor and Emma, but she wouldn't fire anyone without proof of their wrongdoings. She maddeningly thought of Jacob in that moment and felt a pang of regret at her anger for his nonchalance when Ashley and Gabriella were stealing. Lisa heard him out.

"Never even happened like that," he said to her. "I don't dig older chicks anyway." Joan was no help since she had been sleeping, and Lisa was at her wits' end. Lisa knew there was lewd behavior between Helga and Tommy when there was no one else in the shop, but she made it clear that it was invited! She couldn't fire Tommy without hard evidence, which came later that week in the form of Shannon, like Vincenzo, had a habit of sweeping through the back door.

Shannon was a pretty young thing, and she knew it, but wasn't conceited. She was long and lean and looked like Lisa Marie Presley in her hey-day. She had worked for Shear Madness for the longest time, doing facials. Since then, she had gotten her cutting license, but King refused to let her on the cutting floor. Lisa knew the risk that she was taking in hiring her – all of Shear Madness's employees had to sign a contract that they wouldn't cut hair within a ten mile radius. When Lisa mentioned it, Shannon pointed out that she didn't cut hair for Shear Madness; Shannon gave facials. She was alone in the shop when Tommy started his mess.

As Shannon came out of the stock room, Tommy cornered her and muscled her back in with his body language. It was his mistake – this wasn't Helga.

"Hey honey, where you going?" He closed the distance between them so that he was close. She was stuck there with the old Marine. He pawed at her breasts and she pushed him away. Tommy fell into a shelf and was hit on the head by packs of rubber gloves that filled the dispensers on the floor.

"You bitch!" he told her, spitting. Shannon pulled herself back and tilted her chin up.

"Don't mess with me, old man." Was she bluffing? Tommy called it.

"What are you going to do? That old Demato bitch couldn't prove anything and neither can you." Shannon wildly looked around for something to grasp on to.

"If you don't give me a thousand bucks, I'll call your wife and tell her."

"Go ahead, she won't believe you." His bravado was false and his mask was slipping at the idea that the woman might call his wife. Shannon put her nose in the air and sniffed.

"You know you don't want any trouble with your wife, Tommy. Just give me the money and I won't say a word."

"She won't do anything anyway," he said weakly. Shannon could tell that she had him by the balls.

"No, but Lisa will. Say goodbye to your job." She pushed passed him and the rest of the day went along, tense and stiff. Alejandra and Hue exchanged glances with each other as Tommy and Shannon danced around one another with stiff politeness. The other two women could tell that something had happened. Shannon called Lisa that night and told Lisa what had happened and what Tommy had said to her. The next day, she asked him again, and this time he cursed her roundly, refusing to pay anything. Shannon called his wife and received the same treatment. Tommy had already told her that he was a victim of extortion and that she would be calling.

Lisa fired him over the phone that afternoon. The other shoe fell when Ferrari called her that afternoon and told her that he wouldn't be back; she cried hard into the pillow by her bed. Now she was out two hairdressers. Again. And she would have to do more interviews, again. And now there was that same pain shooting up her sides. Again. Was this job ever going to be worth it? And what was next? Lisa made tentative interview with a hairdresser named Jane, and hired her on the spot as she had many others. She was available any time, so Lisa simply filled her name on the list where Tommy had been. Another application brought in Larra, who could come in by train. She put Larra in Ferrari's spot and took a nap with all of her clothes on surrounded by papers.

All was quiet when Anne came in the next Wednesday. She had called Lisa at home and made an appointment with her. Lisa was still cutting hair at nearly nine months, although her days were few and far between. Since she had to be in the salon office on Wednesday's anyway, she decided to go ahead and see her.

Anne was child free that day, and still only asked for a wash and a cut. While Lisa threw the smock around her and cranked her chair back, Anne threw out the first threads of conversation.

"So...I've got this project I'm working on and I want to know what you think." Lisa nodded. Anne did a lot for New Canaan, and had the funding to back it up. She never flaunted it and always volunteered where she could. Sometimes when she came in, she and Lisa would talk about Anne's volunteer work with the community and what she was involved in for that week. Lisa briefly remembered that some of the clients she had *before* Anne knew her through her work, and that it was their children and families that had inspired the look and feel that made little Ieva's haircut a success. Lisa's belly squirmed as her thoughts whirled back to a focus. Anne continued.

"Well, you know I've got a lot of time on my hands with Arnie gone and the kids in school most of the time. I still have Inga, who's more than willing to help out with them, and so I've been putting a fund raiser together for individuals with disabilities." Lisa leaned down and looked at her.

"Arnie left?" Lisa looked stunned. Anne hadn't said anything

101

to Lisa about this yet. Her eyes were guarded but she answered Lisa.

"Yea, he left about a month ago now. He moved in with his sister-in-law." Anne's voice unexpectedly wavered and her eyes filled with tears. Lisa felt alarms racing down her neck and instinctively put her arm around Anne's shoulders.

"Hey, it's alright, Anne, don't fizzle out on me now. What's going to happen?"

"Oh, I don't know yet, Lisa. He's gone and the divorce will be final in just a couple of months, hopefully. I'd like a fast break, but it feels like it's going to take forever. He never was good at compromise, and he's already making a big stink out of visitation with the boys." She dried her eyes, steeling herself and sitting up in the chair. "Jerk," she said, shaking her head mournfully. Lisa nodded and patted her shoulder.

"Enough of that, tell me about this fundraiser of yours."

"Well, it's just a fundraiser, but I thought working with your shop would give you a lot of exposure and hopefully new clients. Now that you are expecting a baby, a few new customers could be a good idea. Are you going to cut my hair?" Lisa realized that she had a pair of scissors in her hand when she was supposed to be lathering her up for a wash. She put them down and put the smock on Anne.

"Sorry," she said, grimacing. "You are in the midst of a divorce and you're worried about me? You know, I've done a couple of fundraisers on my own here with the salon."

"Yea?"

"Sure," Lisa shrugged. "I give haircuts at a reduced price for a couple of days and donate the proceeds to charity."

"I love it. Do you think you could get other salons involved?"

"I could try, Jacob might do it." Lisa giggled. "We could invite Damien."

"And Shear Madness."

"Oh my," said Anne. "So does that work?"

"Well sure, who doesn't love a cheap haircut for a good cause? I advertise a couple days in advance in the paper and the shop fills up fast. Maybe I could call them this afternoon for you?"

102

Anne shook her head.

Anne smiled brightly at Lisa. Just then, her hands flew to her stomach and Lisa almost doubled over. She cried out; pains spidered through her midsection and then receded as quickly as they had come. Anne tried to sit up and take off the smock, but Lisa pushed her back down, holding out a hand.

"I'm good," she gasped. She kicked the release on the chair and Anne sat up, turning around to look at her. Eyeballing her, Anne sat back slowly, as if Lisa was going to explode any second now.

"Who's coming in to replace you?" she asked.

"Huong and then Hue, and then their partner today will be Jane. After that it's Alejandra and Shannon."

"Who's Jane? What happened to Tommy Linguini?"

"He molested Emma Demato and then tried to corner Shannon in the stockroom."

"Are you kidding me?!" Anne screeched.

"No, and then Ferrari walked out. He claimed that the place wasn't fast enough for him and that there just wasn't enough hair for him to cut."

"Wow, honey, and you're about to pop! What else could go wrong?" Anne asked thoughtfully. Lisa spent the rest of the afternoon that day wishing she hadn't said that and rubbing her aching back. Huong showed up as Anne was walking out, and Jane wasn't far behind. At the top of the ten o'clock hour, both of the employees were ready on the floor, but Lisa was trapped in her office on the phone with the IRS and the department of labor. The calls had come in back to back and she didn't know what to do. She opened the door to her office and pointed at the phone for the girls to pay attention.

"No, no, I don't pay anyone any kind of cash," she was saying on her end. She listened closely. "No, they're not technically employed by me, they're subcontracted." Huong could see Lisa's knuckles turning white while she talked on the phone. She wandered back into her office and shut the door. Huong and Jane looked at each other, shrugging. In her office, Lisa put the cordless phone down on the desk, seething. Not knowing what else to do, she grabbed the log book from the podium and called the only person that would know the enormity of the situation or the people involved. The woman on the other end sounded like she was in no hurry.

"Hello?"

"Raheleh called the labor board and the IRS."

"Who is this?" The woman sounded confused.

"Anne, damn it, it's Lisa. Raheleh is trying to report me to the IRS."

"Ok," Anne really was confused now. "Start at the beginning." Lisa told her the whole story, from the time she had left, to the time that she had called. First she had gotten a call from the labor board. Apparently, Raheleh had told them that Lisa fired her because she was Muslim. Lisa told the man that had called that it didn't make any sense, considering that she had two Vietnamese women, a Columbian and a recently fired Italian. She didn't even mention the hot to trot Estonian woman. An hour later, she had gotten a call from the IRS, which is bad enough as it is. She had been reported for paying half by check and half by cash, which she didn't do. On top of that, Raheleh had recounted how Lisa's ticket old system prevented them from making private appointments, and that she was not reporting any of the taxes that she was supposed to.

"So wait," interrupted Anne. "You just said that the IRS told you that it was reported that the way you have things set up won't let anyone make appointments and that you're not reporting your taxes, right? Or whatever?" Lisa got it.

"Right."

"Lisa?"

"Yea?"

"You just started that last week. Raheleh wasn't there for any of that so how did she know that there was a new thing where people couldn't make private appointments?" Lisa's chin fell to her chest when it dawned on her what Anne was really asking. Raheleh wasn't there when she changed the system. She had no way of knowing that the 'employees' couldn't make private appointments. She would have been told. Anne continued.

"Who was here when Raheleh was here?" Lisa thought back. It had been months since she had come and gone. There was Damien, who was gone and had started his own shop. Vincenzo had been there. Gabriella and Ashley were there. All of the people that had been there when Raheleh was there were gone, except one.

"Helga." Lisa said quietly into the phone. She was on the verge of tears again and her back was aching like someone had hit her several times.

"Do they know each other?"

"Yes, of course. When I hired Raheleh, I hired Helga to fill in on the weekends because Ashley and Gabriella were living it up at my expense," she said to Anne. "Raheleh actually recommended her, and at the time, Raheleh was good for her word, so I didn't think anything of it."

"How did they know each other?" Lisa paused a moment and realized that Anne had gone into lawyer mode. Her ears were on and her questions were concise. This was far more than salon gossip.

"I think they used to work together over at this place called Hair Sophisticate. I'm not sure, all I know is that there's no one else that has anything to do with her except Helga. So." Lisa left it at that. It wasn't much, but it would have to do. She chatted a bit more with Anne and hung up. She fired Helga when she walked through the door the next morning and worked her shift herself. As Helga walked out the door, she turned her head over her shoulder and asked why she had been fired.

"Misconduct," Lisa shot back at her. There. Helga shrugged. There was no reason to accuse her of talking to Raheleh, there was no reason to make things worse.

"Figures." Helga left and the bell tinkled behind her. Lisa stayed for the rest of the day and went back to her home, exhausted and anxious. She fell into bed and knew no more, or at least until the pain in her back cranked up to a ten, and she took the ambulance to the hospital.

CHAPTER 11:
WITH A LULL IN BUSINESS

It was six months before Lisa would see Anne again. Lisa had her baby the night that she had spoken to her over the phone and  decided that she should fire Helga. It had been long and difficult, but finally, with a sweating brow and ragged breath, she was holding her beautiful baby. Anne didn't stop coming to the shop even though Lisa was gone; she was as loyal as ever. She came in often and had her hair cut by Larra, who had replaced Helga so many months ago. When Anne came in and saw Lisa standing by the mirror, she was elated. Anne sat in the chair and just turned back and forth for a few minutes chatting.

"How's Joey?" she asked immediately.

"He's good. He's finally sleeping through the night and he's got his two bottom teeth."

"Aww, he's growing up so fast."

"I know," Lisa said sadly. "How's the salon?" Lisa had been there once a week to pay the bills and put out the schedule, but other than that, she had thoroughly enjoyed being a mother and that was it. Anne chuckled and replied, "You don't know?" Lisa shook her head no. Anne replied, "Well, let's see. I usually get my hair cut by Larra. I think she's alright. She talks a little bit too much, but I find it relaxing. Sometimes though, she goes over to another client or stylist and chats them up during a cut, but she does pretty well."

Lisa needed more information. "Is she working out though? I mean, I haven't gotten any complaints. In fact, I'd have to say that she's one of the best I've ever seen. She's a perfectionist." Anne nodded.

"Well, there's a few that will tell you that she's slow, but I like her, like I said. I don't think she's a problem though…I think your real problem is Stacie." Stacie had been there for six months as well.

"What do you mean? What's wrong?"

"Well, she just comes across as…" Anne struggled for the right words. "Thoughtless."

"Explain."

"Well, I was in here one day, and Larra was cutting my hair and it was all fine…then Brenda and Tiffany came in. Brenda asked Stacie her name, and for the life of her, Stacie didn't know. She literally looked down at her shirt to check for a name tag that wasn't there."

"Whoa."

"Right."

"Well, she does a pretty good job with the books. I haven't missed any appointments." Anne smiled.

"I heard you hired an accountant."

"I did. After Raheleh called the IRS and all of that I hired an accountant to take care of the books for me so that I couldn't get in any more trouble."

"You got in trouble?" Anne was ready to get fired up.

"Not exactly. Just the way that I had worked things, there were a few mistakes that I couldn't back up, or find the receipts for, that sort of thing. The things that Raheleh said were dismissed the first day but as protocol they had to continue their investigation. It's alright, and hiring Rebecca was worth every penny because now I don't have the headache." Anne smiled.

"Anyway, Stacie seems like she's had some issues answering the phone too; she's picked up the phone on me and not known what to say." Lisa supposed that this was something to think about, but she couldn't afford to have the hairdressers messing with the client list anymore. Anne liked Larra and didn't want to sell her out, but Lisa could tell that her friend had more to say on the subject. She didn't press it.

"Well, whatever the case is, sit down, and let's get your hair washed and cut before the sun goes down." Lisa was being silly – it was nine in the morning. Anne turned around and Lisa cranked up the chair and pulled the smock on over her. As they got down to business, Jane came in for her shift. She was, as usual, early. Lisa pounced on her.

"Hey Jane, I am really glad that you're here. I was wondering if you'd start opening the shop for me so I can spend more time with Joey and Larry in the morning," she said as Jane put away her things and got her station ready. Lisa liked Jane a lot – she was a great stylist and she cut men's and children's hair as well as women; she was also incredibly dependable and never complained. Jane smiled.

"Yea sure, I don't mind at all." Lisa beamed.

"Great, I'll make you a key." They were discussing what things Lisa would be responsible for in the mornings when a fat, flashy, balding man walked into Lisa's Classic Cuts. He was tall, and he was fat around the middle. His shirt was a silk print, open at the throat with a mat of ugly chest hair spilling out of it and stretched across his big belly. He was bald on top and had a few Charlie Brown strands and a ring of hair around the back of his skull. There were big fat rings on each finger and a huge medallion nestled in the cleft of his shirt. He smelled like cheap cologne that smoked cigars and he walked with a swagger. He pointed a beefy finger at Lisa.

"You the owner of this slum?" he asked her. He had a thick New Jersey accent and sounded like someone named Vinnie. By God, right before her in her own salon stood Colton King.

"Yes, this is my *salon,*" she said pointedly.

"Listen, that bitch Shannon works here, and I know she works here, and if you don't get rid of her, I'll sue the crap out of you. She signed a contract." Lisa wasn't about to get worked up with this guy.

"What does the contract say?"

"The contract says that she can't work in another salon doing facials within ten miles of here."

"Shannon doesn't do facials." King sniggered and strode around her shop sneering and sniffing at her décor. "Boy this place is a dump," he said to her. Lisa felt the top of her head getting hot while Jane and Anne just watched.

"In fact," Lisa continued, "Shannon doesn't even work here." It was a bold lie, but why not? If he could come in and insult her salon and her senses and her nose, then why should she let anyone be subject to his classlessness?

"Bullshit. She's been seen. Another employee seen her sneak around the building and through the back doors, so don't deny it. I couldn't prove Vincenzo came in here and butchered people's heads off, but I've got people watching the place now, so don't lie to me." He stuffed his thumb into his chest and puffed it out. "I'm important, I cut TV hair, and I don't want my employees slumming with you and your white trash, scumbag, wanna-be stylists."

Anne looked at Lisa for a reaction. This disgusting creature was in her salon, insulting her stylists, cursing up a storm, and had the nerve to call *her* trash. Was she going to say anything to him?

"I'd appreciate it if you'd show a little decorum in my *salon*," Lisa said with dignity. She straightened up her spine.

"No more class than those two broads you left outside your *'salon'*." King put mocking emphasis on the word salon and threw two fingers in the air to make quotes. "Yea, I saw them outside. I saw Bleachy Baby out there with her dingbat buddy sitting on the sidewalk waiting for someone to let them in. That's bad for your image, babe." He took another look around.

"Well," he said. "I didn't come to sit and chat, I came to tell you. Leave my employees the hell alone and get rid of whatserface or I'll sue the shit out of you. I'll be sending a certified letter letting you know that I mean business. I would like this building though; it would make a great addition to my *salon*." With that, Colton King turned on his heel and left. Anne shook her head. Lisa had to restrain herself from punching the counter.

"Man, I hate that guy," was all she would say for the next hour while cutting hair. Shannon was on her way out the door, and Lisa hated it. She was worried about what King had said about Larra and Stacie. She didn't understand. Larra was the quintessential California girl – bleach blonde hair and a weathered tan. She wore shorts a lot and had long, tan legs. Stacie on the other hand, was older and had black hair with plenty of gray roots showing through. Lisa had offered to color it for her, but Stacie had laughed it off, saying that she chose to grow old gracefully. When Jane told her that King had a point and that someone else had complained to her about them sitting outside, Lisa was furious. She remembered having to come unlock the door for them, but never had she heard the insults that were being slung around about her employees. Was she not paying attention that day? They had looked alright to her, but then, Lisa was rather forgiving. It didn't matter. Somehow, it just didn't matter. The letter came and Shannon's days were numbered. Lisa approached Huong again about going full time.

"No," Huong said shaking her head vehemently. Her eyes filled with tears. "No, in fact, I may have to stop altogether." Lisa waited for her to continue. Huong looked at her with the saddest eyes she had ever seen.

"I'm pregnant," she announced sadly. Lisa was surprised. Huong had been complaining that her husband was gone a lot, and that he was a hard-nose who didn't do that great a job taking care of the kids. "I can't take full time." Lisa's heart fell. Hue had left a month earlier, claiming that while she enjoyed cutting hair, that her clientele wasn't "rich enough" for her.

"My kneecaps aren't being rubbed the right way," Hue had told her. So Lisa, severely disappointed, had let her leave. Lisa was shocked back to the present by Huong's voice.

"I know someone else," she said.

"Another Vietnamese girl?"

"Yes, this time her name is Chi, and she's the same age as Hue."

"23?" Lisa said pointedly with her eyebrows raised. Yes, Lisa had known that Hue had lied about her age – but the Woman Code prevented her from saying anything about it. Besides, who cared? Hue was an okay hairdresser and that was all that mattered to Lisa. For all of her employees, Huong and Hue had been a loyal, if not entirely lethal pair of cutters. They didn't cheat her, they didn't lie to her about the business, and they didn't steal. Lisa was happy. Huong laughed at Lisa through her tears.

"No, Chi is in her forties, 46, I think. Her husband is like Hue's also; he is a lawyer. She doesn't have much else to do, so perhaps she could work full time."

"Well we'll call her and see. Are you quitting?" Lisa knew how hard it was to be pregnant and work full time – she had done it.

"No, I don't think, yet. We obviously need the money."

"Yea," Lisa understood. Joey was six months old, and Lisa knew that it must be three times as hard with more children than that, especially infants. She took Chi's number and promised that she'd call her in the morning. She also sent Huong home to rest – it would prove to be a slow day and there was no harm in it. In the meantime, Larra was due in the shop in an hour.

Larra came in that day complaining about the train.

"It's so slow," she said. "I wish I had a car." Lisa's nose wrinkled when Larra came close. She smelled like a brewery. She had admitted to Lisa that she had a drinking problem, but she had told Lisa that she only drank at night while she was alone. When Lisa had asked her why, Larra told her the story of her life.

"Well, in the 80's, my husband and I had our own salon in Westport. He was the love of my life and I loved my job and my salon. It was a lot of hard work but we stayed open from 7am to 9pm, and people would come in and get cuts that were out of this world. " Lisa was impressed. She knew what kind of work it took to run a salon first hand. Larra continued.

"In 87, he contracted Leukemia and from there it took six months for him to pass away. We did everything the doctors told us to; he took the pills, he did radiation, he smoked weed to combat the radiation, and in the end, it didn't even matter. He died before he reached 35. It just happened so fast. I guess I died a little too, I don't know." Lisa, who was of course, married and pregnant at the time, was moved to tears. As she reflected back on it now, she could feel her eyes filling up again. She couldn't imagine being without Larry or feeling so alone in the world. She pressed her hands to the side of her temples and warded off the emotions that threatened to take over and fixated on the complaints about the train.

"How long will it take to get your driver's license back?"

"I've got two more classes and then I've got to pay off the fees and I'll be back on the road."

111

"Great, I can't wait. You ready to start today?" Lisa wanted to leave, but Larra didn't know that just yet.

"Sure!" Larra said to Lisa. She sounded a little wobbly, but she looked ok otherwise. Lisa went back into her office and Larra settled into her station. Anne came in while they were both there. She sat in Larra's chair and as soon as Lisa heard her voice she poked her head out of the office.

"Hey, you traitor!" Lisa exclaimed to Anne. Anne smiled at Lisa; she was already in the chair with the smock on and the water running behind her.

"Oh, stop. I'm so loyal to this place if it closed down I'd move you into my office." It was true – loyalty in the world of hair was everything. Lisa tapped her chin thoughtfully.

"So, have you thought more about the cut-a-thon idea?" Anne snapped her fingers.

"Yes, I have, and the more I think about it, the more I like it."

"Ok, sounds good. Larra, what are you doing?" Larra, who had been silent most of this time was chopping away at Anne's hair. It was much shorter than it should be. Lisa hadn't been paying attention and Huong was long gone.

"I'm cutting Anne's hair. Look," she said, turning Anne around to the mirror behind them.

"Christ," said Anne. She briefly closed her eyes and then turned away, struggling to get out of the chair. "It's cut enough." She wasn't as angry as she was when Destiny had messed up her hair, but she was definitely disappointed. She hopped out of the chair and gathered up her pocketbook, paid for her haircut and left without another word.

Lisa left Larra alone on the floor, until she heard someone speaking aloud in the salon.

"Hello?" a voice called out. Lisa poked her head out of the office and there was a gentleman standing there waiting for someone to come out. She washed her hands in the sink and sat him in one of the chairs.

"No one came out when you came in?"

"Nope," he said, shaking his head. "You're the first."

"Ok, hang on," Lisa said. She went into the stockroom and

looked around, and then knocked on the restroom door. She pressed her ear to the door and heard Larra talking in the restroom. Who was she talking to? It was a single restroom. Lisa could hear that there was only Larra in there and she was talking to herself. She shook her head and banged on the door. There was no response, but she could hear her.

"Larra, are you alright, honey?" she asked her. There was no answer. Lisa banged on the door. Lisa could still hear her talking to herself inside the restroom. She banged on the door again.

"What?" groused Larra.

"Are you ok in there?" asked Lisa.

"Yea, sure," Larra slurred back. Lisa left it alone and returned to the cutting floor.

The client in the chair was waiting patiently and Lisa came out to apologize.

"It's ok, I understand," he said, smiling. "I'm still a pretty good tipper." Lisa laughed and trimmed his hair just above the ears like he wanted. He was still there when Larra came out of the bathroom, leaning slightly to the side. Her backpack was dangling off of one shoulder. Lisa was alarmed.

"Why don't you go ahead and take a lunch," Lisa said. Larra often went to Club Sandwich for lunch and stayed for the entire hour, unlike most of the stylists who brought their own lunch or supper. It wasn't often that she didn't go out – and she always took her backpack with her everywhere – to the restaurant, to the bathroom, and back again. It dawned on Lisa right then. Larra was drinking in the bathroom. She waited for her to come back.

When Larra did come back, she looked a little better. She was walking a little straighter and seemed to be a little brighter. She wasn't slurring – as much. Lisa didn't know whether or not she should approach her now or not, but she knew that she couldn't let Larra work while under the influence – especially since she had butchered the hell out of one of her best customers. She decided to give Larra the benefit of the doubt.

"Larra, I noticed that you were walking a bit funny, are you ok?" Larra glanced at Lisa.

"Yea, I got hit by a car a while back and this old back just hasn't been right since." Lisa eyeballed Larra for signs of intoxication. Since she had called Larra out, Larra had straightened her spine and watched her gait so that she looked normally functional.

"You got hit by a car?"

"Yep."

"You lived through it?"

"Yea, it really only clipped me and it wasn't going very fast," said Larra. "I'm alright for it. Had to have a little bit of physical therapy, but I didn't lose much." Larra swirled her soda in the can she had and took a sip. Lisa felt a migraine coming on and let it go. There would be other days. Besides, she had to get a packet of paperwork ready for Chi, whom Lisa had called and was coming in the morning and Larra only had an hour before Jane would come in to replace her. Larra drained the rest of her drink and screamed, dropping the can. Lisa was confused. Larra was waving her hands and pointing at her tongue. She screamed more, and stuck her tongue out at Lisa. Her tongue was swelling and she was crying. Lisa shook her.

"What happened?"

"Uh bhee, shthers uh bheeshting od muh thung." Lisa looked at her soda can and sure enough, there was a wasp crawling around on the lip of it.

Lisa called the ambulance and they came to investigate. Larra wasn't allergic to stings, but there was no telling what would happen if her tongue kept swelling.

When Jane came in that afternoon, Larra was loaded up and the ambulance was pulling away. After that it had been slow, but reasonable, and Lisa had been able to make a few phone calls. Stacie wasn't there to man the phone today – after the incident with that blowhard Colton King, she had shaved off some of Stacie's hours, and so she was scheduled for the times when the salon phone was the busiest. Jane, who was competent and a decent hairdresser, took over the salon for Lisa and she felt confident going home.

Chi came in the next day, on Saturday. When Lisa had called her, she said it was the only day that she could work.

"Why Saturday?" asked Lisa during their interview over the phone.

"Because I like to be home when my two children get home from school," she had told her. "I have two kids, a boy and a girl, and they are both school aged, so I like to be there." Lisa knew that feeling, even though Joey was still at home.

"Huong said you had a license, why don't you cut hair professionally?"

"My husband is wealthy, and I don't really need to work, but I like to keep my skills up."

"Oh, really?"

"Yea, I've been licensed for some time now. My husband looks at it, he thinks it is silly, but I don't care." Lisa liked Chi a lot. She was personable and kind; and she knew that Chi would fit right in. She hired Chi on the spot and told her to come in the following Saturday. She didn't know it, she would need Chi more in the future than she did right now.

CHAPTER 12:
MORE CLASSIC STUNTS

It was a slow day and it was Alejandra and Huong in the salon that afternoon along with Chi. Alejandra was complaining about the lack of customers that day.

"So we won't eat meat this week, pasta still fill you up." said Chi, who always had a positive attitude about the lulls in business. Huong on the other hand, had complained bitterly at the lack of business. She was entirely dependent on the clients to come in. She started to cry, and Chi and Alejandra scoffed at her as she sniffed into a tissue.

"I can't help it," Huong said tearfully to Chi. It was Saturday.

"You're crying like a big baby, what's wrong with you?" Chi and Huong had been at each other's throats all morning, and Alejandra was tired of it.

"She's pregnant," Alejandra said out of the blue. Huong gasped and Chi nodded wisely.

"That makes sense," she said. Huong looked alarmed.

"How did you even know? Did Lisa tell you?" Alejandra shook her head.

"Honey, no one tells me anything, I just know. You cranky, you hungry, you crybaby," she said in her thick Columbian way. "Then you throw up everywhere. Alejandra knows." Chi nodded at her also. Huong had run to the bathroom that morning when she opened a fresh bottle of Barbercide, a potent cleaner that they used to disinfect combs at the salon. Huong looked miserable.

"What am I supposed to do, I cannot afford another baby" she wailed, leaning on the broom. Chi spoke up.

"Give it to me." Huong looked shocked.

"What?"

"We got plenty of money. We would adopt it and you'd be free of your little problem." Chi said it so nonchalantly that you'd think she was being cruel if you didn't know her, but Chi wasn't like that. She cared about everyone, and it showed in her work; as a result she had built up quite a clientele of her own that would likely follow her. When small children would come into the shop she would go the extra mile to make them feel comfortable – just as Lisa had with Ieva. For the girls, she would put little barrettes or little balls in their hair after a cut, and for the boys, she would often give them an extra lollipop for being good. Lisa had heard nothing but good things about her, and Chi was as loyal as any employee that Lisa had ever had. For her to ask to adopt Huong's baby was as natural as daylight and Alejandra nodded approvingly. It was true too; they had enough money: Chi's husband was a wealthy attorney in the United States and they had amassed a nice sum of money over the years that they had been in America. Chi drove a luxury car and their family lived together in a huge mansion in Ridgefield, a town 30 minutes away filled with other huge houses that belonged to other wealthy people. Huong considered it, and nodded.

"I'll think about it, Chi. I know that you'd only want the best for my baby and my family." Chi nodded, and the conversation was dropped when Larra came in looking for Lisa. Alejandra gasped when Larra took her sunglasses off. She had a huge shiner as black as night.

"What happened?" Chi asked. She and Huong exchanged glances. They already knew. Larra didn't reply, only asked for Lisa. She was off that day, so she scribbled Lisa's cell number on the back of her hand and left. None of the women said much about it after that. The day passed uneventfully. When Lisa came in that afternoon, she brought her son Joey, and the playpen. She set it up in the corner and it was well uneventful until she closed that night.

She flipped the closed sign over the door and went to her office to make phone calls. The first person she called was none other than the great Orv Byron.

"Hey, Orv, it's Lisa!"

"Well hey there, gal, it's good to hear from ya!" He sounded genuine. "You ready to give up and come on back?" he said chuckling. He knew full well she wasn't coming back; it had been almost seven years.

"No, Mr. Orv. I was actually wondering if you wanted to participate in a fundraiser. My friend Anne is holding a fundraiser to benefit students who receive special education services."

"So, it's for their education or what?"

"Not exactly, it's actually for our education. SPED*NET New Canaan is about teaching people how to resource information on behalf of people with disabilities."

"Well, I guess that sounds alright. What do I have to do?"

"All you have to do is do what you do best," she said teasingly.

"Stand here and look handsome?" Lisa laughed out loud at him.

"Yes, exactly. Seriously, all you have to do is show up and cut hair, and for every haircut you give, you donate the proceeds to the fundraiser."

"I can do that," he agreed.

"Really? So I can count you in?"

"Sure."

"Yes!" she squealed. "Thanks, Mr. Orv."

"You know, there's still time to come back and cut hair for me. I sure could use someone dependable and talented." Lisa blushed, though he couldn't see it. Orv didn't hand out compliments like candy, so when you got one, you cherished it, and she did.

"Thank you."

"You're welcome, honey, I hear from some folks that you're doing a fine job. Keep it up, and you might just be all right." She hung up the phone glowing, and as it turned out, the five other businesses that she called for the cut-a-thon all wanted a piece of the action as well, each armed with two or three hairdressers that would be glad to volunteer. She couldn't wait until she saw Anne again. When she did, it was three weeks later.

"Anne," she said that afternoon as soon as Anne walked in the salon, "Guess what?"

"You sold your horse to a farmer and you're moving to Florida to sell ice cubes."

"That's not it, and no."

"Well?"

"Oh! Um, I called around about volunteers for the cut-a-thon."

"A-a-a-nd?" She drew it out because she knew Lisa was trying to keep her in suspense.

"I have nine hairdressers and three barbers that are ready to cut hair for you." Anne's mouth dropped open. She wasn't expecting that.

"Really?! That's so great, thank you!!" Anne did a little dance there in the salon. She was more excited than ever about the project. She sat in the chair and waited for the smock to go around her. Lisa obliged and they got down to the hairy business of salon gossip.

"How's everyone?" she asked Lisa.

"Fine, so far. I saw what you meant about Stacie not having it all together. I asked her to hand me the log book yesterday and when I looked in it, it was nothing like it was when she first started working for me."

"Not doing as well?"

"Well, now there's missing appointments and things in the wrong place, and all kinds of misinformation. I can't help but wonder what she's doing up there. I was thinking about letting her go, but I can't think of anyone else that I know that would be able to replace her and I don't want the rest of the hairdressers to have access to my client list." Lisa thought briefly about Destiny. She didn't want anyone having her client list ever again, if it meant anything. Anne nodded.

"Makes sense. How's Larra's bee sting?"

"She's alright. She should be here in about fifteen minutes." As the time passed and Lisa put the finishing touches on Anne's hair, she realized that Larra still hadn't come in. It had been an hour. Anne left, and Lisa was left wondering. Lisa called Jane to fill the void. It was three days before she would hear from anyone regarding Larra again, and when she did, it was the police. A uniformed detective came in and approached Lisa. Jane and Alejandra were working that day, and Lisa left them on the floor and pulled the detective into her office.

"What's going on? Is there something wrong?"

"I understand that," he flipped open a notebook, "Larra Fisher works here?"

"Yes of course; is she alright?"

"Ma'am, can you tell me about the last time she worked?"

"She came in and worked, and then left...she's d been drinking at work and I had to speak to her about her problem, but otherwise, she came in and left just the same as any other day."

"What time did she usually get off?"

"I had Larra working till about 8pm so that she could catch the train back to Stamford."

"So she left here last Wednesday? And didn't come in on Thursday?"

"Right."

"Lisa, I'm afraid that Miss Fisher was robbed and raped as she disembarked the train last Wednesday. She was almost killed and she's still in the hospital now." He waited for Lisa to react. She didn't fail him.

"Oh my god!" she cried, clutching her chest. "Is she alive? Is she alright? What about her boyfriend? Was he there?" She spat the questions at him, rapid fire.

"Well, I can't disclose much at this point, but she asked the department if we would reach out to you. I'll let her know we spoke and you would like to speak to her when she's able to call." Lisa grunted. Sure he would.

"Alright then." He was scraping his chair back and getting ready to leave, then shaking her hand and walking out the door. She was numb from the encounter. She called Jane and added a couple of more days to her schedule and then called the newspaper to run an advertisement for another hairdresser. A woman named

Jean answered the advertisement and as usual, Lisa hired her as soon as she could work.

The shop over all was doing well, and Jane was as dependable as ever. There was one slight issue with her, but with a little time, Lisa thought it could be overcome: Jane had a problem with self-esteem. When she cut someone's hair, she would ask: 'Is it ok? Do you really like it?' And of course they did, she was a fantastic hairdresser, but you couldn't tell her that. When Jean came, they would argue bitterly over clients that would come in. One afternoon, Alejandra called Lisa furiously on the phone.

"You need to fire these people!!" she said angrily. Lisa had never heard her sound so angry.

"What's going on?"

"They are fighting over clients! One of them walked out and the other one just stood there confused, but I tell you the clients both wanted to leave, and I don't blame them. They are fighting; it's petty childish drama." Alejandra was usually pretty quiet, but Lisa knew that she wouldn't be much longer if she didn't do something to break the two of them up. She decided to come down there herself and survey the scene. That didn't work, of course; as soon as the boss showed up, they stopped fighting. Alejandra, at least, was pleased to see her, but the other two worked in a dour silence. She didn't stay long, and Alejandra didn't call her again. Huong, however, did. She was not a bearer of good news.

"I have to quit." She said it quietly, as though she were embarrassed.

"You're pregnant, I know," said Lisa.

"Well, you know Chi offered to adopt the baby, right?"

"I had heard, but it wasn't my business."

"I decided that no matter what my money looks like, I can't give up my baby. My husband and I talked about it, and he thought it was a good idea at first too, but he changed his mind too." Lisa nodded on her end of the phone. She understood. There were times when she was pregnant that she was scared to death, and almost willing to give her baby up for adoption. But she, like Huong, was made of sterner stuff than that.

"That's good, Huong, and I know how hard it can be to make

121

a decision like that, especially when it looks bad. Do you think you could do two more weeks?" Huong said that she could, and they hung up with each other, both happy. Lisa would find someone in the meantime.

Despite the petty fighting, Jean was doing well at Lisa's Classic Cuts. Lisa had known Jean for some time, and it was this reason that she was reluctant to hire her. She did though, and it seemed to be working well. Jean had been part of Gabriella's crew during hairdressing school, and had been in trouble for driving under the influence. She was also out of work, and couldn't seem to hold a job, which Lisa knew were two big red flags; she had ignored them both.

"I'm much better than I was, and I'm just taking things one day at a time," she had told Lisa. Lisa couldn't argue with that, so she hired her. Jean had been calling for years to try and get a job with Lisa, but finally, in a moment of complete desperation she hired Jean against her better judgment. Lisa was in her office one afternoon when a customer knocked on her door, furious. When she spotted what was the matter, she almost gasped against her will. The man had the most awful haircut she had ever seen.

"Look what she did to me!" he exclaimed. "Is this how you run things?"

"No, of course not!" Lisa cried. The customer softened towards her, leaning in as if to conspire.

"Lisa, listen. I told her three times that she was doing the wrong thing. She ignored me the first time and insisted the second two times that she was doing what I had told her to do. I knew she wasn't because I could feel the draft on the back of my head in a place where there was supposed to be hair." He looked kind of sad telling her all of that. Lisa was heart sick.

"Ronnie," she said to him. "It's Ron, right? Ronnie? Look. She's off tomorrow. Your haircut is on the house, and she's off tomorrow. If you come back, I'll fix your hair myself for free."

"You know that I'll be back," he said kindly. "But she won't be cutting my hair ever again." Lisa nodded, and couldn't blame him. That afternoon, she spoke to Jean.

"Jean, we need to talk about the customer you had this

afternoon."

"Oh, that jerk that wouldn't let me finish the job?"

"That 'jerk' is a regular customer, and you did a hatchet job on his head. I can't have customers walking out of the shop looking like that." Lisa could feel the top of her head getting hot.

"That's stupid, he looked fine." Jean's voice was becoming shrill and loud.

"Don't raise your voice to me; I saw what walked out of here and I felt so bad for him that I've offered to fix it for free."

"You didn't have to fix it," she insisted. "Whatever he said to you was a lie." Lisa sighed. She wasn't interested in arguing with Jean, but she knew that Jean was full of utter crap if she thought that she had given a decent haircut that afternoon. It wouldn't matter.

"I did have to fix it, it sucked." Lisa was flat out pissed off.

"Excuse me?"

"I said it sucked." Jean turned red in the face.

"You don't talk to me like that!" she countered hotly.

"YOU DON'T JEOPARDIZE MY BUSINESS!!" Lisa roared back. Jean was awestruck and Lisa turned on her heel and slammed the door to her office. Neither one of them spoke for the rest of the afternoon. When Lisa came out of her office she approached Jean.

"If you send another customer out of here looking like Ron did today, I will fire you." Jean just nodded. She apologized the next day, but Lisa kept her eye on Jean from then on out, cutting her hours and scheduling her when Lisa worked. Jane and Jean continued to fight, although Jane managed to keep it under wraps while Lisa was around. Jane closed the shop that night and Lisa left. She had an early appointment with Anne in the morning, who wanted a haircut before she had to be at court.

As she pulled her car into the tiny parking lot that morning, she was greeted by Alan, the landlord of the salon. Lisa juggled coffee and bagels in a paper sack while she got out; he grabbed her breakfast and waited for her. She was worried that something had happened overnight. Alan was an incredibly responsible – he owned the lawnmower shop in the plaza across the street and others down the street. He had a habit of strolling by and checking on Lisa's salon at night before he went home.

"Is everything ok?"

"Yea, yea; I…uh…hm." He sighed. "I saw some lights on in your shop last night, and I walked over to take a look." She waited for him to continue. She realized that he was blushing.

"What?"

"Well, I saw one of your stylists on the floor…um…make…um, making love…"

"What?"

"I believe it was Jane, and I'm pretty sure that it wasn't her husband." Lisa's mouth dropped open while she listened to Alan recount the scene that he had saw the night before. She was appalled, and wanted to giggle so bad she could feel it bubbling in her gut. She could see Anne pulling into the parking lot and told Alan that she would handle Jane. Anne met Lisa by her car as Alan was walking away.

"What was that all about?" she whispered to Lisa.

"I'll tell you when we get inside," she replied, handing her the bag of bagels and a coffee. As she reached to unlock the door, she realized that Jane was already inside – or she hadn't left, whichever was which. She smiled at Jane. Jane's eyes looked red and her smile was watery, as if she had been up all night.

"What are you doing here so early?" asked Lisa.

"Ah, well, I couldn't sleep so I just came on in."

"Alright," said Lisa smugly. "Listen, do me a favor and go to Costco for me, and pick these things up." Lisa pulled some cash out of the till and handed it to her. Lisa gave her a list of things that she needed for the shop and sent her out. The list was long and she wouldn't be back for a while. As soon as the door had tinkled behind Jane's back, Lisa turned to Anne with a bagel in her hand.

"Alan caught Jane screwing on the floor. Wasn't Derek."

"What! Stop it," Anne screeched.

"Yep, I'm serious."

"Oh my gosh, is that why she's still here?"

"I think so, but I haven't said anything yet to her obviously."

"Are you going to?"

"Of course."

"Wow."

"I know." Lisa suddenly started to giggle and couldn't stop. Anne caught the fever and before either one of them knew it, they were struggling to breathe. Anne wiped a tear from her eye and Lisa clutched her stomach. As she straightened, she remembered that she was here to cut Anne's hair.

"Come on, hop in the chair and I'll give you a trim." Anne stepped up into the chair and Lisa threw the smock over her and sprayed her hair with water. As she cut, Anne snickered and Lisa almost lost it again. Jane came back as Anne was leaving and Lisa didn't waste any time.

"So, Jane, Alan said that he came by last night and saw that you were here after hours. Was there something wrong?"

"Uh, no, I just left some scissors and I came to get them. It's my only good pair."

"You didn't stay?"

"No, of course not." Lisa looked at her smugly. Jane blushed. "Well maybe for a little while."

"Jane, Alan saw you." Jane looked at Lisa and Lisa just sat back and let the words sink in. Jane flushed a dull red.

"Lisa, I'm sorry," she said, her eyes filling with tears.

"Look, this isn't a hotel, it's a damned salon. If you're looking for a thrill, look for it somewhere else, because this isn't the place. This is Lisa's Classic Cuts, not Lisa's Classic Sluts."

"Yes ma'am." Jane whispered. Lisa left Jane on the salon floor and when Alejandra came, Jane knocked on the door.

"What's up?" Lisa called out. Jane timidly opened the door.

"Lisa? Look, I'm sorry…and I've decided that it's better if I go."

"Wait, what? Come on. I didn't fire you."

"I know, it's just…I'm so embarrassed."

"Jane you're a great hairdresser, you just made a mistake that's all. You're forgiven. Now get back to work." Lisa was close to begging. She couldn't afford to lose her. "Please?"

"No, I'm sorry. I just…I can't. I've done you really dirty, and I just…I can't work here anymore. I can't face the landlord, I can't face you. I'm really sorry." Lisa shook her head and Jane gathered

125

up her stuff and left. She tried to push it out of her mind and worked instead, on organizing her part of the SPED*NET New Canaan event. She had to get ready. Her mind drifted along with her paperwork, and before she knew it, she was napping on top of her desk.

Alejandra held the door open for Lisa when she came in one Saturday with a box full of stuff. She smiled.

"What's in the box?" Alejandra asked curiously. Her curiosity was satisfied when a fluffy white kitten poked its head over the

side of the box and mewed at her.

"Oh! Look at the baby!" Alejandra exclaimed. Lisa smiled and handed her the box.

"Here, you take that, so I can set him up in the rest room." Alejandra took the kitten out of the box and Lisa pulled out a litter tray and a bag of litter. Along with that she took a small bag of food and a double sided bowl and put them on the counter. She filled the litter box and the food bowl and put them both in the bathroom, closing the door.

"Where did he come from?" asked Alejandra. Lisa took the kitten from her and put it in the salon bathroom.

"Well, Jean said that she wanted a kitten and my neighbor has a whole litter of them that she is trying to get rid of, so I promised Barb that I would bring her one. What do you think?"

"I think she got what she wanted," Alejandra said, shrugging. Lisa laughed. She didn't care; she was just being nice to Jean. Lisa had called her but she wasn't due in for another hour. A regular client came in to get his haircut in the meantime. He was there every Saturday and got the same haircut every time.

"Hey Brian," she exclaimed when she saw him. He sat in the chair and waited for the chair to empty, picking up a magazine. It wasn't long and Lisa was ready for him. He saw the kitten tottering out of the restroom and they started to chat about it.

"Man, what a cute kitty! Is that yours?"

"Nah, I'm bringing it in for Jean, she said she wanted it."

"Well that's nice of you. She coming to get it today?"

"Yea, she should be here in a little while." Lisa snipped away at Brian's hair and finished quickly. He was good for a trim, but that was about it. He commented again how cute the kitten was and left, tipping Lisa fatly.

Jean came in a few moments later.

"Here kitty kitty, oh, Lisa, Thank you!" Jean's face was shining and she was smiling from ear to ear. While she called the fluffy white kitten, it didn't appear. The smile slipped away from her face and she looked despondent.

"Where is it? I thought you said you brought it," she asked Lisa accusingly. Alejandra raised her eyebrows.

"I did," said Lisa. "I'm sure that he's around here somewhere."

"He's not here, he's not here!!" she cried. Alejandra rolled her eyes and grabbed a broom.

"Come on, Jean, we'll look for him." Lisa hunted in the bathroom and in the stock room to no avail. Alejandra went to the front door and closed it all the way, making sure that if the kitten went towards it, it would not be able to get outside. Then she cleaned out the two other cubby holes of their supplies to make sure that the fluffy white beast was not in any of the boxes. Jean scoured the restroom; she looked behind the toilet and in the cabinet under the sink – she knew that a curious kitten is quite the acrobat. She followed Lisa into the stockroom after she left and called for the kitten. The group searched and searched but no one could find the kitten. Jean's eyes filled with tears.

"What happened to it?" she wailed. Lisa felt so bad. It couldn't have gone anywhere. No one had gone out the back door, and since Shannon didn't work there anymore, it didn't need to be unlocked.

"I don't know," Lisa said. "It was just me and Brian and he left right before you came."

128

"He took it then!" Jean cried.

"No, he did *not,*" replied Lisa.

"Yes, he did. Give me his number so I can call him."

"Absolutely not."

"Give me the number! He stole my pet!"

"He did not steal your pet, it's still here somewhere. I'm not giving you my clients' phone number so you can call and harass them for something that he didn't do."

"Fine!" Jean shouldered her way past Lisa and Alejandra and snatched the log book off the podium. She flipped through the pages until she had what she wanted and ripped it out of the notebook. Grabbing the phone, she dialed the number. When Lisa reached her hand out to take it from her, she turned away. Furious, she went back into her office to flip through applications. She was tired of it. She heard Jean leaving a message on an answering machine.

"Yes, this is Jean down at Lisa's Classic Cuts; this call is for Brian. Brian, if you could call back right away, it's an emergency. Please call us immediately, as we have reason to believe that you've stolen something that belongs to me, thank you." She hung up the phone and paced the salon. Alejandra was still looking for the kitten and Lisa pulled out some prospective employees applications while they looked. Ten minutes passed and she could hear Jean on the phone again.

"Hi, this is Jean at the salon again, if Brian doesn't contact me right away, I'll be calling the police to report my property stolen. This is your last warning." Lisa shook her head and emerged from her office. The kitten hadn't been found, and Jean was becoming distraught. She held out her hand for the phone and Jean snatched it away again. She hit the redial button and pressed the phone up to her ear once more. When the phone rang this time, she could hear a woman on the other end answer. Not only was she being loud enough to hear the entire conversation, but she was angry and you could tell.

"Who is this?" asked the voice.

"This is Jean, at the salon. Your husband had a haircut here this morning and then proceeded to walk off with my kitten."

"My husband is allergic to cats, and there's no way in hell he would steal."

"You're lying, and he's got my cat. I'm calling the police and having you arrested for catnapping."

"Let me talk to your boss."

"She isn't here." Lisa scoffed at the lie. She shook her head.

"Well, we don't have your cat, and don't call here again, or we'll have you arrested for harassment." Lisa heard the phone click in Jean's ear. Lisa held out her hand for the phone and Jean dissolved into tears. She paced around the shop. The phone rang in Lisa's hand and Jean scooped it out of Lisa's hand before she could answer it.

"Hello? Yes, this is Jean. Oh, hello, Brian. Yes, I think that you've got my cat." Pause.

"All of a sudden Jean's voice got extremely loud, "You were the only one in the shop! It was just you and Lisa. All of a sudden, the cat disappears. I know you stole and kidnapped that cat!" Brian raised his voice and you could hear him too.

"I do *not* have your stupid cat, lady, and I would advise you to stop calling my house and talking to my wife, or I will have you arrested for harassment." The phone clicked again, and Lisa was ready to fire her. Just then, the kitten came crawling out of the stockroom, meowing. It walked right over to Lisa and twined itself around her ankles. Lisa pointed at it.

"This your cat?" she asked Jean. She clapped her hands together.

"Yes! Where have you been!!" she said, scooping it up. Alejandra followed the kitten out of the backroom and pointed behind her.

"I found him in the backroom underneath the shelf where Lisa keeps the foils." She said it so matter of factly that Jean flushed.

"Lisa, I'm so sorry." Lisa shook her head.

"I'm not the one that you need to apologize to."

"What do you mean?"

"Man you need to call that client back and apologize to him for making an ass of yourself."

"No! Do you know how badly embarrassing that is?"

"Of course I do," she roared. She rarely raised her voice. "You jeopardized my client and my business, you used my phone to call him up and harass him about something he didn't even have, and now you're refusing to apologize."

"Ok, ok! I'll call him in a couple of days; give him time to cool off."

"No, you will call him now. In the meantime, I'm going to go ahead and put another hairdresser on the schedule."

"I'm sorry."

"It's fine."

The rest of the day was uneventful. She interviewed a beautiful Costa Rican immigrant named Evita, and another woman named Robin. Evita actually had a portfolio and while her accent was pretty thick, she was an excellent hairdresser. She was coming from Sharkey's Cuts for Kids, which meant that she had plenty of experience, but she hadn't liked it because she was paid a wage and tips. Lisa paid by commission and that was much more lucrative when you brought your own clients, as most of the hairdressers Lisa hired often did. Evita had her quirks, of course. She was an open lesbian with a wonderful girlfriend that always packed her lunch for her. Evita was always pulling out a big bowl of fried rice and Lisa often wondered how exactly she kept her lithe figure.

"I go home and work out for hours," she had told her. She was fairly nice, and Lisa had thought that she had hit pay dirt with Evita until she too, showed a deficiency in sanity. It happened one quiet afternoon when Evita couldn't find something in the cubby of her station.

"Where is it?" she muttered in her thick accent. She was pulling things out of her station and dumping them on the floor.

"You ok?" asked Chi, who was working that particular Saturday.

"It's not here, I left a Snickers bar in my cubby hole and now it's missing." She knocked on Lisa's door.

"Have you seen my candy? I left it here last time I worked." Lisa shook her head.

"I try and stay away from the stuff, it's bad for you. C'mon I'll give you a Cliff Bar instead, I even have Kind Bars," she offered.

"No, I want my candy bar." She asked Chi. "Have you seen it?"

"Nope," Chi told her. "Haven't seen anything of the kind." Lisa could see that Evita was getting upset.

"Evita, have you looked everywhere?" asked Lisa.

"Of course I have looked everywhere, do you think I am stupid?" Lisa looked at her strangely and shook her head, shrugging. Evita was about to lose it when a light bulb went off over her head.

"I know!" Someone stole it and I know who it was! It was that cleaning woman that you hired to come in here at night!" Evita pointed her finger at Lisa. Lisa looked aghast.

"What? Come on!" Lisa couldn't believe it. "Well, my god, why don't you call her if it's that big of a deal. She doesn't speak much English though, so good luck. Why don't you just write a note for her and leave it for next week."

"No, I will fix her. In my country when people steal your food, you kill them."

"What the hell, Evita, this is America. You can't kill someone for stealing a candy bar." Evita sat down on the couch with her drink in her hand. It was a Steaz tea, which was green tea that tasted like soda. It was a darker color and mixed well. Evita guzzled it down and walked to the sink to refill the empty bottle with water.

"What are you doing Evita?" Chi asked her.

"I will fix her," she growled with her thick accent. She poured Barbercide into the rest of the bottle. "I'll leave this for her and she will steal it and die." Lisa almost shrieked at her.

"You can't do that!! Let's just ask her if she took it and let her buy you a new one."

"No, I will fix her."

"Evita." Lisa's face must have been turning red, because she could feel it. Chi was backing away slowly.

"No, I will fix her." Evita sat on the couch in the salon and rocked back and forth. "I will fix her," she muttered over and over. Lisa tried, with futility to convince her that it wasn't square to kill someone over a candy bar here in the United States. Finally, at her wits end, she pointed at the door. A brief memory flickered into her mind.

"Evita, pack your scissors and get the hell outta here!"

"I will fix her good!" she said, still rocking as if she hadn't heard.

"*GET OUT! GET YOUR STUFF AND GET OUT OF MY SALON.*" Lisa was quickly losing her temper, but a sudden hand on her arm stalled her fury out. Chi was still there. She patted Lisa on the arm.

"Just tell her to leave," Chi said. "No reason to lose your mind, too." There was reason number 4,278 why she was incredibly lucky that she had hired Chi to begin with. Evita had already started gathering up her things and was getting ready to leave, so Lisa just went to her office and slammed the door. She came out later and gave Chi a huge hug before she left after her shift. Alejandra came in that afternoon and got her station ready. Lisa regarded her thoughtfully.

"Alejandra?" she asked. "You're not going to just up and go psycho on me some day are you?" Alejandra laughed at Lisa.

"Nooo," she drawled. "I am as normal as I can get, considering."

"Considering what?" Lisa asked with a raised eyebrow.

"Considering that I work in a salon with a bunch of sillies." Lisa burst out laughing and laughed until she collapsed on one of the salon chairs. Somehow, it would all be alright.

CHAPTER 14:
I WANNA ROCK N ROLL ALL NIGHT – AND CUT HAIR EVERY DAY!

Lisa was napping again in her office chair two weeks later when the phone rang. The day had come and gone, and as she  peeked out of the tiny window in her office she realized that she had slept for a couple of hours. She had finally gone back to work, and while she and Larry were making it, things were difficult at home. She had been doing that a lot lately; the long hours and baby at home were taking its toll, and often she'd end up locked in her office while the salon floor was covered by the other girls. Lisa often laughed that she was taking a leaf out of Joan's book. It was expected, however, and she was working the transition from hairdresser to "Super Hairdressing Awesome Mom." The phone rang again and she picked it up.

"Lisa's Classic Cuts, Lisa speaking."

"Lisa it's me." It was a soft voice on the other end of the line, male and unassuming. She almost didn't recognize it, but it clicked.

"Gene?" The voice laughed.

"Yup!"

"Hey, man, how is it?"

"It's alright, I guess. I've been staying with Mom and Dad again. It's not that great, but hey, it's a place to live."

"So you're here, then?"

"Yea." Gene and Lisa had grown up in Norwalk forever together. Their dads had been best friends and even though Lisa and Gene had been several years apart in age, they grew up together as good friends.

"Wow, what are you doing these days?"

"Well, I got into another accident a while back, so, not really much," Gene laughed. Lisa's brow furrowed on her end of the line. He had already been into two accidents, one that he shouldn't have walked away from but did.

"A car accident?"

"Yea, I got rear ended; messed up my neck and my back really bad. I mean, I was messed up before, but this one really got me. It wasn't even that bad of an accident, but I guess my body just kinda gave up on me. I got a hundred grand out of it though, so for that I can't complain."

"Didn't you have herniated discs or something?"

"Yes, I had had surgery on it before, remember?"

"I do."

"Anyway, I stayed with Mom and Dad to recoup this time, and God they're as awful as ever." Gene always complained about his parents – especially his mother. They were strict and tried their best to keep Gene on a tight leash. Whenever he would find a woman that was interested in him, Gene's mother would always find a way to get rid of her. "I want to get a job and go back to work."

"You're cleared to work?"

"Sure. Doctor said that there's plenty that I can do, I just can't do any major lifting and running, or whatever. I'm fine."

"Well, what kind of work are you doing these days?"

"It just so happens that you kind of inspired me. I am a licensed hairdresser now." Lisa shrieked into the phone.

"Are you serious? Excellent! Do you have any specialties?"

"Yes, I like coloring and cutting women's hair, and I do some kids, but you know how that goes." Kids didn't really like Gene – he was tall and big, and kids were afraid of him. His French and Italian ancestry gave him long thick curly hair that looked like a long afro. It didn't deter him though. Lisa liked the idea that he was a hairdresser. Gene paused on the line and waited for her to speak, and when she didn't, he started.

"Sooo...."

"Yes." Lisa already guessed that Gene wanted a job. She had

known him a long time.

"Really?"

"Absolutely. I need you as soon as possible. Are you available this week?"

"Doctor tomorrow, and then I'm free."

"Awesome. I'm on Forest Street, you know where that's at?"

"Oh yes. What time?"

"Be here at nine a.m. and we'll get you started. Bring your papers so I can make copies of your license and all of that."

"Ok, boss lady."

"Stop it." Gene snickered.

"Sorry." They said their goodbyes and hung up with each other. The next day, there was Gene in all of his glory, standing there in front of the shop with Alejandra, waiting to get in. Lisa had gone home and dug something special to wear out of the closet. When Gene saw it, he nearly fell apart.

"You didn't!" he said, hugging her. "I can't believe you still have that old thing."

"I would *never* get rid of this," she told him. Alejandra, who had been chatting with Gene, looked confused. Lisa was just wearing a beat up denim jacket, as far as she knew. When Lisa turned around to show her the back, Alejandra let out a low whistle. The back of Lisa's jacket was painted with the album cover of Ozzy Osbourne's "Ultimate Sin." It was mostly orange, as if a depiction of hell, complete with a demon that had Ozzy's face and a buxom woman looking over her shoulder with vengeful red eyes. Alejandra shook her head and sighed.

"Silly," she said to Lisa. "Beautiful work though, did you paint that?" she asked Gene.

"I did that years ago when that album actually came out. It wasn't that popular but I liked it."

"Nice work," Alejandra commented. "If you cut hair as good as you paint; you'll do fine." Gene and Lisa smiled at each other and they got down to business. She showed him where to put his stuff and got him started in his niche. A couple of hours dragged by and Lisa sent Alejandra out to Costco to get paper supplies as she had Jane do before. Alejandra didn't mind, there wasn't anything going on, and Lisa usually found a way to compensate for the loss if it got busy while she was gone. Gene paced nervously back and forth as they waited for someone to come into the salon.

"Is anyone coming in today?" he asked her.

"Sure, I mean, this is one of our slower days, but I thought it would be ok for your first day. I didn't want you to get overwhelmed."

"Well true, but gosh, I wish there was something I could do here." Lisa smiled with understanding. She thought about it and patted the back of her hair, looking in the mirror.

"I could use a trim and some hi lights," she told him. "I could pay you for that, if you really want something to do that badly."

"Oh, Lisa, I would love to do that!" Gene took Lisa's hand and led her over to the chair at his station. He put on the charm.

"Well, hello there ma'am. I'm Gene and I'll be your stylist today." He bent and kissed her hand. Lisa rolled her eyes and jerked her hand away.

"Stop that, silly." Gene snickered and threw the smock over Lisa and set her chair up to his height. He sprayed her with water and got to work on her trim.

"Just a couple of inches, ok?" she told him. As he snipped, she tried to catch up on the gossip with Gene.

"So, weren't you married before?" Gene almost wilted.

"Yes. I married this Russian woman with a little boy. It didn't work out, but I almost didn't leave anyway. We were living in Stamford for a while."

"What happened?" Lisa asked.

"Oh god, she was gross. She didn't clean up after herself and the house was a mess. She didn't bathe that often so she smelled, and she totally ignored her son, who was the sweetest boy you could ever imagine. If it hadn't been for Alex, I would have left a long time ago. I felt bad about leaving him there alone with her. He'd basically been raising himself."

Lisa felt bad for the boy. She understood what it was like to be a single parent – more and more Larry was gone while she was at home with Joey, or Joey was with her mother while she worked. Time was passing quickly, and the boy who it seemed was just born yesterday was well on his way to being three. She turned her thoughts back to Gene.

"So why did you leave then?" she asked him.

"She cheated," he said bluntly. "I'll put up with a lot, Lisa you know I'm a nice guy, but no. Not that." Lisa didn't blame him. "I filed for divorce and that was the end of it."

"Wow," said Lisa. "Is there anyone else?"

"Well, you know how Mother is, so I've taken to dating online. I'm sort of seeing this woman from Tennessee ."

"Oh, is she nice?"

"Yes, I like her a lot. She's been through it, and she says that she's scared because she's been beaten up by her old boyfriends and crap like that. So I told her, "Hey – I'm not into that at ALL." Gene was telling the truth, and Lisa knew it. He was a gentle giant.

He pulled out the supplies that he would be using to color her hair with. He laid out the foils and the powders and got started on the top of Lisa's head.

"Don't you think you should be putting the highlights in the back?" she asked him.

"Sure, don't worry about it. He mixed the solution and carefully applied the foils, this time, to the back of Lisa's head. Much better, she thought nervously. As she sat there, she noticed that Gene had used 40-weight bleach when he should have used 20. While the time passed, she felt something in the pit of her stomach – the foils had already been on there too long. She looked at Gene, who had his back turned to her, and was wiping the counter. He swayed on the spot, but didn't know that Lisa was watching him.

"Hey there, are you alright?" she asked him.

"Sure, why?"

"Well, because I'm watching you and you don't seem very steady on your feet. Are you on medication or something?" Gene looked chagrined.

"As a matter of fact, yes I am. I'm on pain meds for my neck and my back."

"You should have told me that."

"I was afraid that you wouldn't give me a job."

138

"Rinse this mess out of my hair so I can turn around and yell at you!" Lisa was kidding, sort of. She just really wanted the foils out of her hair. Gene obliged and turned her around so he could work on the back of her head. She could feel the bleach starting to tingle. As Gene rinsed her hair out, she could literally feel the strands breaking off.

"Gene, what did you do?" She lifted her hand to try and feel the back of her head and he pushed her hand back down.

"I didn't do anything, but there's something wrong back here. It looks like your hair is uneven with the highlights because of the last stylist you had, I'm guessing." When he turned her around, she looked at her poor hair. It was fried. This wasn't good. The color was uneven, although the foils had been applied correctly. The ends were breaking off and it just looked completely awful.

"Gene," Lisa said delicately. She was looking for a nice way to chew him out. "No, never mind. Just rinse me, but we've got to figure out a solution to the problem, because other people's hair is far more important than mine...we'll get an egg timer or something."

"I'm sorry." He looked upset. "I guess I just lost track of time because of the meds."

"It's fine." Alejandra chose that time to walk in. Her arms were laden with bags of paper towels and new combs. She looked at Lisa's hair and Lisa shook her head minutely. When Gene left the two of them alone, Alejandra got cranked up.

"Did he do that to you?" she asked her pertly.

"Lord, yes. He's on medication for his back and he left it in too long."

"You think he'll do worse on someone else? You're the owner!"

"No, we'll get him a timer. He just lost track of time that's all."

"Bad for business, mami." Alejandra held no loyalty to Gene, but she cared much about what happened at the salon.

"I know. He'll be alright."

"Oh, we need to talk, by the way."

"Don't do it to me, Alejandra."

139

"I have to. I have to go back to Columbia for a while."

"How long?"

"I'm not sure, my father is very sick. My mother needs help."

"Well, we'll be here. There's always a spot open for you in the shop." Alejandra smiled at her.

"I'm going to arrange for it in two weeks so that you can get two or three stylists to replace me." Lisa laughed and rolled her eyes. She hugged Alejandra and knew that it was best that she go. Not that Lisa wanted to hire someone else. But family was family, and that was the secret to running a good salon too – you treated your clients like family, you treated each other like family, no one could complain. When the phone rang in the salon, Lisa picked it up. Stacie had long been fired uneventfully, but Lisa was back in action so she was able to take care of most appointments and phone calls that came through. Besides after Jean and her incident with the cat, she kept the appointment book close at hand. The woman on the phone had a thick accent and Lisa's stomach sank when she realized who it was.

"Lisa."

"Raheleh, what do you want? You can't come back here to work."

"Please, I need something."

"After all that you've done? Didn't you call the IRS and tell them that I was doing something wrong? Yes, you did. You defaced my car; you embarrassed me in front of clients. I wouldn't give you a job even if I could." Lisa pointedly noticed that she did not deny any of the accusations. Lisa made a mental note to start parking her car in front of the shop where she could see it.

"I don't need this from you. I heard you were putting your salon up for sale." It was true, and yet it was gossip. Lisa had considered putting the shop's lease up for sale and moving across town, but there had been no decisions made. If rebellion had anything to do with it, she would die on Forest Street and have her body put on display in the front room just to tick her off. Lisa was *that* angry. She felt almost like baiting Raheleh; Lisa was only curious as to what stupid thing would come next.

"And?"

"I will buy it from you and you will move away. You will not work in this town anymore; it will be in the contract."

"I wouldn't sell you a glass of ice water if you were in Hell and on fire." Lisa rarely said mean things, but Raheleh was teetering on a nerve that was already frayed.

"Then give me a job."

"You're not welcome here, don't call me again." Lisa hung up the phone without another word from Raheleh. Lisa was normally a nice person but there was no love lost between them, and there was no remorse in her heart when she turned Raheleh down and hung up in her. Alejandra just looked at her with raised eyebrows and shook her head. As the clock ticked by that day, it was time for Gene and Alejandra to leave. Lisa decided that it would be a good day to leave early, so she did. That afternoon, she booked an interview for the next morning, and called Anne. When Anne got on the phone, they chatted about the upcoming event.

"So what have we got so far besides the cut-a-thon?"

"Well, it's looking good. I've got a few sponsors as far as things like kids' activities and whatnot. I spoke to the town managers and they said that we could use Irwin Park for the day. Bounce About is going to donate a bounce house for the kids and possibly a dunk tank, but I haven't decided yet. It still might be cold. I figured that we could either sell tickets or charge fifty cents or a dollar. Then we've got a couple of volunteers that want to paint faces and run mini games. I'm trying to think of something else that might draw people in. I want this to be huge, to let people know that we really are about something special."

"What about food?"

"I'm still working on that one."

"Well, you could charge for tickets to the mini-games and let them pay for food."

"Hey, that's a good one."

"What about a cutting floor?"

"I think that what we'll do is get some tall chairs. You said you had nine others?"

"Eight, plus me."

"Ok. We'll get some tall chairs and if you'll come in early on

141

that day, you can help get set up. I'll need everyone to bring their own smocks and stuff."

"Sure, and I'll bring the ones for the kids as well."

"Great." Anne and Lisa were well on their way to getting the event established. A light bulb practically shattered over Lisa's head.

"How about a celebrity impersonator?"

"Who?"

"I know someone who does a great Gene Simmons."

"Really? That's the guy from KISS, right?"

"Yes. This guy does a great one. I know him personally, you'll love him."

"Are you sure that it's a good idea for a disability fundraiser?"

"Probably not, but it couldn't hurt. The adults might like it."

"Good point. Ask him and we'll talk about it."

"Ok, got any more ideas?" Lisa didn't and they chatted for just a few more minutes before they hung up. The event was in six months, so they had plenty of time to get ready. Lisa gathered up her purse and locked the door firmly behind her. She got out to her car that was parked at the curb in front of the shop and nearly dropped her bag.

"God! No!! Come on!!" Lisa didn't realize that she was shouting, or that she was waving her arms. The only thing that she could concentrate on was the giant scrape on the side of her car. She circled around it two or three times before she noticed that there was a business card attached to the windshield. It was for the landscapers that had their office in the same plaza as the landlord's lawnmower business, and there was a cell phone number scrawled on the back. She opened her car door and sat down in the driver's seat to make the call. A man answered.

"Hello, I got your card on the windshield of my car. Did something happen?"

"Sure, I'm really sorry. One of my employees hit your car today while he was trying to squeeze through with the trailer. It sounded like there was no way he could have avoided it. I am really sorry."

"Well, I've got to call my insurance company before I leave

here. Should I get your information, or the companies, or his?"

"Hmm, see that's the reason I left my card, I wanted to talk to you about it. See, there are some people that work for me that aren't exactly…"

"Legally supposed to be here?" Lisa filled it in. There were a lot of Latino gentlemen that worked for the landscaping company, and other construction businesses in New Canaan. Most of them didn't speak English, and although it wasn't directly stated, it was likely that most of them were illegal immigrants. The man on the other end of the line sighed.

"Yes. And if you report it to the police or the insurance, I'm going to be out a crew foreman. However, I don't want you to be upset or without a car, so I'm willing to pay for the whole thing in cash if you're willing to not report it." Lisa scowled on her end of the line.

"That could cost thousands," she said to him.

"I know. I saw it. But it's worth it. This guy is good, he works hard, and his crew never has any complaints…and I don't speak Spanish so if he leaves, I'm screwed." Lisa sighed. As a technicality, she really had him over a barrel. If he was being honest, he would pay and get her car fixed. If he was bluffing, she could just report him to the police and her insurance.

"Alright then, I'll let you pay for it. What do I do?" The man let out a sigh of relief.

"I'm going to give you a phone number for an auto body shop that my company uses. They know me; I'll call them and tell them to expect your call. Make an appointment, let them fix it there, it might take a couple of days if you can stand that. If you need a car, tell them that you need a loaner and I'll make sure that's covered too. Tell them to bill Daddy Watchel; they'll know what to do. I'll make sure that I let them know you're going to call. I promise they'll take good care of you." Lisa couldn't argue, so she promised to call that afternoon and make an appointment.

Lisa went home and called the auto body shop to make her appointment. The woman that answered the phone knew exactly who she was and made her appointment for the following Friday. Larry was angry that she had agreed to let the company cover the

143

damages to her car, but Lisa didn't understand what the big deal was as long as the car was fixed. The night ended in an argument with Larry about something that Lisa couldn't even put her finger on. She thought about calling her mother, but instead, she tucked her baby into bed and cried herself to sleep.

CHAPTER 15:
YOU MUST BE JOKING, RIGHT?

The week dragged by. Gene was doing well at the shop, although Lisa had found that he had a bit of difficulty blow drying

hair. He wasn't that great at monitoring the dryer and didn't want anyone to get hurt. She decided that she could tag team with him the way she had with other stylists on multiple color jobs and it was working out well. She had also asked him if he was willing to attend the SPED*NET New Canaan fundraiser as Gene Simmons and he agreed that he would. His messy afro was just perfect for the job, he told her.

Lisa had an interview and hired a new barber to replace Alejandra. Alejandra's time was counting down very quickly and Lisa knew that she would be difficult to replace. She still had Jean, although she was teetering on the edge as usual; she still had Chi, who would come in on Saturdays. Things at the shop, over all, were fine. Things were falling apart at home, however. She called her mother on the way to work.

"Can you help me out? I need someone in the shop to take calls for me. I could pay." Lisa sounded dull and tired.

"That isn't what you called me about."

"Yes it is."

"No it isn't, tell me what's wrong."

"There's nothing wrong, Mother," she said with a note of annoyance in her voice.

"I hate it when you lie to me." Lisa's mother let her comment hang in the air and gather momentum as she waited for Lisa's reply.

"I asked Larry to move out and told him I wanted a divorce."

"Oh honey." Lisa had to pull over in her car, which was due at the body shop in an hour. "Please support me on this, Mom," she cried into the phone. "We always argue and I just can't take it anymore." Lisa's mother was very frank in her next statement.

"He doesn't deserve you. You deserve better." Lisa sighed into the phone. Her mother spoke again, changing the subject.

"What time should I be there?"

"I have to drop my car off at the auto shop and then I'll be there to open, so come in at about ten, I guess." She sighed again.

"Mom?"

"I love you too, honey."

"Thanks." She hung up with her mother, got back on the road, and headed to the auto shop. She took her keys inside and started the intake process. The woman behind the counter was an older lady of about fifty, with coiffed blonde hair that Lisa knew was well taken care of. She greeted Lisa warmly, and very nice, for which Lisa was grateful.

"Hi, you must be Lisa. I'm Rochelle, and I'll be making all of your arrangements. Come on in and have a seat over here." She led Lisa over to a desk with a computer on it, and seated Lisa opposite her. She handed her a paper to fill out and Lisa started scribbling immediately.

"Ok, I've got to get you to fill this sheet out, and ask you some questions, and then you'll be ready to go." A side door opened then, and a uniformed employee came in with dirt and grit on his fingertips. Rochelle pointed at him.

"That's Gary; he'll be helping take care of your car. If you feel ok with it, you can go ahead and give him your keys and he'll pull your car around to the shop. You can get your stuff out of it and whatnot in a few minutes." Lisa smiled and dropped her keys into his palm and he nodded with a smile and walked out to the lot where she had left her car.

"Now, let's get down to business. Lisa Maria, right?"

"Yes." Rochelle motioned for the sheet that Lisa had filled out.

"Good, good." She perused the sheet. She entered the information into the computer, and as she got down the page, she stopped.

"You're a hairdresser? My daughter just graduated from beauty school." Lisa smiled at the old term and nodded. "She

146

needs a job really bad," Rochelle continued. "But she isn't really looking."

"Oh?" said Lisa.

"Yes, she mostly sits on my couch and watches TV. I wish she'd do something." Lisa had a clenching feeling in her gut. She thought she knew what was coming.

"What salon do you work for, so I can mark down your work information?"

"I own Lisa's Classic Cuts, on Forest Street."

"Oh, you *own* your salon? Wow, my daughter really needs a job." Rochelle was trying to sell her on it. Lisa smiled.

"Let's finish this first, and then talk about it." The older blonde agreed and the process was sped up. Rochelle even gave her the keys to a loaner car before Lisa asked for them.

"Now that's out of the way," Rochelle said. "Can we talk about a job for my daughter?" Lisa smiled wanly.

"Sure. I could kind of use someone," Lisa admitted. "Is she dependable?"

"Well, I trust her to run my errands, and when I work late, she makes dinner. She keeps to her appointments and whatnot." Lisa nodded. She wondered how many more times Rochelle would say "whatnot."

"Have you seen any of her work?" Rochelle patted her perfect hair and pointed her index finger at her hair.

"You're looking at it. I let her practice on me all through beauty school." Lisa did have to admit that Rochelle looked good. Lisa dwelled on it for a moment. It was the third of October and people would soon be filling the shop – the holidays were coming and everyone wanted to look good so it was a busy time of year. She could definitely use the extra hands, and Lisa thought that if the girl could make her mother look that good, then surely she could bring some extra money in.

"Alright, you got me. What's her name?" Lisa asked.

"Her name is Camber Lehman."

"Ok, tell her to come in tomorrow at 10am, dressed for an interview and then I'll make my final decision." Rochelle did a little dance in her seat and shook Lisa's hand. Then she led her through the side door that Gary had come out of earlier. Lisa's car was already in the shop, but she could see that it was in line behind two others. She got her things out of it and Rochelle sewed up the rest of their contract.

"Don't you worry about a thing, honey. Your car will be good as new in three days' time; I'll call you when it's time to come pick it up." She smiled and tugged Lisa's sleeve as she walked her to the loaner car. "And thanks." Lisa smiled back.

"No problem." By the end of it all, Lisa had forgotten all about her soon to be ex-husband and was looking forward to going into the salon. Her mother was already there and sitting at the podium taking calls. Gene was there, and he was cutting a woman's hair while her daughter cowered across the room looking rather small on the sofa in the salon. Gene loved children, but they sure didn't love him – at least until they realized that Gene was about the same age at heart as they were.

The noontime lulls in business made Gene bring out his comic books, which Lisa enjoyed looking through too. When the new barber came in at three, Lisa was surprised, and had forgotten all about him. He pulled up in front of her shop on his bicycle, carrying a backpack on his back. Lisa's stomach sank a little. He didn't look like someone arriving at work – he was sweaty and out of breath from riding. Lisa couldn't say a word. He shook her hand.

"Hey Lisa, thanks again."

"No problem, Kyle. If you want to get set up over here, you're more than welcome." She pointed at an empty station, and Kyle smiled. He held up a finger.

"I've got to change before I get started; I don't want anyone to smell me." He went into the bathroom and came out wearing a clean shirt and smelling nice. Kyle really was a snappy dresser. Lisa motioned to the bike, which he'd left outside.

"You can park that over in the corner if you'd like," she told him. There was just enough space for it, she believed, and as it turned out, she was right. While they discussed it, Lisa's most favorite customer came in for her bi-monthly haircut.

"Anne!" said Lisa. "This is Kyle, my new barber, and this is

Gene, who works as a stylist." Anne nodded to both of them and smiled. Lisa introduced her mother and Anne tried to stick out her hand but Lisa's mom waved it off and gave Anne a big hug instead. Anne liked her already. She looked around.

"Should I try out one of the new guys?" she asked Lisa. Gene smiled and patted his chair but Kyle looked nervous.

"No, I think Gene's about to go on lunch, actually, and Kyle here specializes in men's cuts and children's hair." Kyle breathed a sigh of relief. He had told her that he felt slightly uncomfortable about cutting women's hair, and Lisa had needed someone that could cut men's hair confidently. With Alejandra leaving and Gene being a hairdresser that had his preferences, Lisa was a little stuck. Kyle had rolled in at just the right time. She tugged on Anne's hand.

"You sit with me, silly." Anne smiled.

"I want the works." Lisa looked impressed.

"Hot date tonight?"

"I wish. Court with Arnie tomorrow. I've got no idea what kind of stunts he'll pull tomorrow."

"Well, at least you'll look nice." Anne smiled.

"How's Joey?"

"He's fine." Lisa didn't elaborate and could feel her stomach clenching up. Lisa saw her mother shoot a look at her out of the corner of her eye. She got up from the podium and went into the stock room, motioning to Kyle.

"Let me show you where things are, Kyle." Lisa knew that her mom was giving Lisa a few minutes alone with Anne – her mother didn't know where anything went in that stockroom. Kyle and her mother went into the back of the salon. Anne didn't have a clue.

"How's Larry?" Boom. There it was. Larry. Lisa took a deep breath.

"Larry and I are getting divorced." Anne's mouth dropped open and she whipped around to look at Lisa.

"Really? No way!" She was appalled. Anne knew first hand that divorce was awful. It felt like you were carving away a part of yourself that you had known that was familiar. It hurt like nothing else in this world. Her eyes filled with tears.

"Yea. I told him I wanted a divorce that day I called you on the phone about the cut-a-thon."

"Jeez, Lisa." She was silent for a moment. The silence was broken by Lisa's mom shepherding Kyle out of the back room.

"Bathroom's over here," she said, pointing. Lisa smiled. Good ole Mom. Anne smiled through her tears, and Lisa fixed Anne's hair so that it was perfect for court. Lisa hugged Anne before she left and kissed her on the cheek. The rest of the day passed without event for either of them. Lisa closed the shop and drove home again in her loaner. Her mom would not come in the next day – she was making arrangements for Lisa at a nearby daycare for Joey, one that was closer to the salon. In the meantime, Lisa was on her way to work where she was waiting for her interview.

At first sight, Lisa felt that Camber had it all together. She had dressed sharply in a business suit and flats. Her hair, much like Rochelle's, was blonde and fantastically cut. She had brought her license papers in with her, and her resume and even a tailored cover letter. Camber had even brought her equipment to show Lisa that she was ready to work. It was a good thing, too, because Lisa hired her on the spot. She really had it all together and Lisa noticed that she was quite confident in her abilities. Lisa put her on the schedule and she started that week along with Kyle and Gene.

Everything was almost fine until Gene dropped a bomb on Lisa. He was doing well in the salon and hadn't had a lot of complaints, although "out of it" seemed to be a phrase that got tossed around a lot. He was a capable hairdresser and still a wonderful friend. Gene had agreed to be Gene Simmons from KISS for the fundraiser, but it was in that momentum that he ground the gears to a screeching halt.

"I'm moving to Tennessee." Lisa's eyes rolled back in her head with shock.

"Man, what? I thought you were going to stay here and help me with the fundraiser, and work for us here at the salon." Gene heaved a great sigh.

"I was, but I really like this girl."

"Is there any way that you can…wait?"

"I don't think so. I mean, I love playing in a KISS tribute

150

band, but it's not so great sometimes." Lisa snorted, and she could feel her temper getting cranked up at her old friend.

"Not so great?" she retorted. "Then why do you sign autographs as 'Gene Simmons' and *conveniently* forget that you're doing an impression? You know? Aren't you the one that told me that people approach you in public while you've got your make up on, but you don't bother to correct them do you?"

"Lisa," he said weakly.

"No! Don't you 'Lisa' me! You made a commitment, damn it, you owe me this! You ruined my hair!!" She was madder than a cat in a roomful of rocking chairs. Gene waited for her to finish and then promptly knocked the wind out of her sails.

"I think I love her." Lisa sighed. What could she say? Sure, she was mad...but hey. Love was love, and she knew better than anyone that you couldn't stop it or take it from someone. She crossed her arms over her chest and Gene came over and bear hugged her.

"Please don't be mad," he begged. Lisa stood on her tip toes and looked him in the eye.

"She'd better be worth it," she said to him. Lisa shook her head and slugged him in the shoulder. He chuckled and rubbed the spot that she'd punched. Camber was due in that afternoon and Lisa would ask about more hours. Unfortunately, she didn't have the chance, because Camber came in and started sneezing almost immediately.

"I have bad allergies," she said between sneezes. Her eyes were watery and blood shot. Lisa handed her a box of tissues that she gratefully took from her boss' hand. "Must be something in the shop," she muttered. It was worse the next day, and Camber called into work. Lisa had to admit that she sounded awful. She wished her well and let her have her day off. The whole first week was like that, with Camber calling in sick every other day. The week crawled to an end on Friday, and ended with a surprise visit from hell. When a uniformed officer walked into the salon carrying a clipboard, Lisa's heart dropped. The police force rarely came to Lisa's for a haircut, although she often gave them discounts. He waited politely to be acknowledged.

151

"Yes, can I help you?" Lisa asked him. "Do you need a haircut?" He smiled at her.

"No, thank you. You're Lisa?"

"Yes, I am." She was almost sweating.

"I've got some papers here for you, if you wouldn't mind signing for them."

"What is it?" she asked as she took the clipboard.

"It's a subpoena. You'll have to open it to find out the details, but I'm here to make sure that you received the paperwork and were legally notified." She handed the clipboard back and the officer left. Gene looked up from his client and over her shoulder.

"What is it?" he asked her seriously. Lisa opened the envelope and read the papers inside. Then she laughed out loud. Gene looked confused.

"It's a subpoena for a court case that involves Helga and Raheleh. Remember I told you about the Iranian woman who freaked out in front of the salon? And the other one that told her everything that went on here in the shop and let Raheleh call the labor board? Yea, now they're fighting." Gene raised an eyebrow.

"The subpoena calls for me to testify on behalf of Helga Ainso against Raheleh Babakan, who is suing Helga for not paying her wages and racial prejudice."

"What are you going to do?" Lisa snorted at Gene's innocent question.

"I'm not going to do anything. It's not my problem. I fired them both, and I don't care."

"That's not very nice." Gene smirked and Lisa shook her head. She rustled the papers and looked for the lawyer's names on the letterhead. She picked up the phone and pled her case to the people that answered. An hour and a half later she had a written response to the summons, and the lawyers were willing to release her from the docket. After what had happened to Lisa's car and with Raheleh and then Helga at the salon, there was no way in hell Lisa was going to testify to anything. Two weeks passed without further notice. Gene left for Tennessee and Kyle and Camber were there in the shop with Lisa. All was well and then the sky opened up and dropped another bomb on Lisa's head, this time in the form of Anne on the telephone.

"Lisa, I had an appointment today." Anne said it without preamble. She wasn't angry, but her curiosity was rampant. Lisa was a stickler about the appointments, especially Anne's. Loyalty was everything, and Anne was loyal, so Lisa returned the favor, whether she was on duty or not.

"Yes, I know. What are you waiting for, you're almost late." It was nearly 11am.

"I can't, my favorite salon is closed."

"What do you mean closed?" Lisa was confused. The shop had been open for hours, and Kyle was supposed to be there any minute. Lisa hadn't planned on coming back until the afternoon.

"I mean it's closed. I went, the door was locked and the welcome sign was flipped to closed and everything. There's a big note that said Camber went to the doctor taped to a trashcan next to the glass door. Kyle pulled up about the same time on his bicycle because he's supposed to be at work in half an hour. I told him I would call you so he went for coffee."

"ARE YOU FREAKING KIDDING ME?! This is the busiest season of the year!!" Anne had to pull the phone away from her ear to keep her hearing intact. She had expected this reaction. Lisa was furious, because this information meant three things exactly: First, there was no one on duty at the salon, and there was no telling how long there hadn't been. Second, it meant that Camber had left without calling her and that was grounds for being fired and third, it meant that the front door was locked, but the back door was *not*. Camber didn't have the keys to the front to lock it from the outside, and the only way for her to go out was through the back door. Lisa sighed.

"Are you busy?" Lisa asked Anne.

"I have a thing at two o'clock, but not really. What do you need?"

"Go through the back and lock the door, and then unlock the front door for Kyle when he gets back. Don't unlock it till he gets there. He's never long. Tell him I said to go on and get his station ready and turn the sign around. I'll be there in half an hour." In her anger, Lisa forgot to say goodbye, but Anne smiled instead. For

153

whatever reason, she felt a swelling of pride in her chest. This is what her loyalty had earned – the trust of one woman's entire business. Anne went in and Kyle returned, relaying the message. When Lisa came in, she came with her lunch and ate with Anne before she cut her hair. When Anne left, Lisa took Camber off the schedule until Lisa spoke with her face to face. Then she put another ad in the newspaper.

CHAPTER 16:
WHAT A MESS!

When Lisa finally did speak to Camber face to face, Camber apologized profusely for the blatant disregard. She told Lisa that she had started sneezing so badly that she had an asthma attack and went to the emergency room. Lisa asked to see her discharge papers and Camber actually produced them, so she gave the young woman a second chance. Nearly a month without a call out or an incident gave Lisa a comfortable feeling, although as anyone could tell you, it was spoken too soon. She got a call from Camber exactly a week before Thanksgiving while she was at work.

"Lisa?"

"Yes, Camber, is everything ok?"

"Yes, I just wanted to ask where the tissues are."

"They're in the stock room next to the paper towels and stuff on the left. You sure you're ok? Do you need to leave?" Lisa didn't want her leaving the salon wide open EVER again.

"No, no. I just need to put out some more paper supplies." Lisa nodded on her end of the line.

"Ok then, Kyle should be there in a little while, and I won't be far behind."

"Great!" Camber sounded happy. She hung up with Lisa and it was Kyle that called her an hour later. It was like déjà vu.

"Lisa?"

"Hey, Kyle, is everything ok?"

"Yes, are you coming in soon?"

"Sure, what's wrong?"

"Well, I was thinking that maybe you should get some more

155

paper towels and tissues and stuff."

"What? I just went two days ago. They can't all be gone already."

"Well, Camber left the dispensers empty, so I went back there to get more and there aren't any."

"Are you kidding?"

"No…" Kyle trailed off. He wasn't much of a joker. In fact, he was usually antsy, serious and something of a nervous wreck. He was rather tall and thin, with wiry hair and a pointed chin. His personality was dominant however, and he liked being busy. When the shop was not busy, he would clean, and when the cleaning was done, he would pace back and forth through the salon. He drank a lot of coffee, but more than one client had suggested substance abuse to Lisa. She refused to believe it. Lisa sighed on her end of the phone.

"Sure, I'll pick some up." She hung up and when she got there, she realized that the place had pretty well been cleaned out. She looked at Kyle.

"It was like this when you got here?"

"Yep." Camber had taken all of the supplies and loaded them into her car before she left the salon that day. There was no way in hell that she was going to work there, or anywhere else if she decided that she was going to put Camber down on an application as a reference. She wasn't done yet, however. Two hours later came the coup-de-grace.

"Lisa's Classic Cuts, Lisa speaking," she said into the phone.

"Hi, this is Ronald Parker from the Fairfield County Health Department. We got a call regarding your salon, and there are a few issues at hand that we need to discuss with you." Lisa groaned inwardly, but proceeded in a professional manner.

"Sure, what's wrong?"

"Well, like I said there are a few things. It's reported that you're running a salon and you don't have the proper supplies – no cleaning agents, no paper products, and that there are airborne allergens around the salon."

"None of that is the truth, although I would admit there's no paper products as of about an hour ago."

156

"What does that mean?"

"An employee named Camber had her shift today and took all of my tissues, all of my paper towels, and everything that was on the stock room shelf in the back. So, no, we generally don't run a salon without paper products but here we are."

"Well, that's not all." Lisa rolled her eyes.

"Oh there's more?" she asked. Her patience was wearing ultra-thin.

"Yes, we looked for your health permit and there doesn't seem to be one. You can't run a salon without the proper permits."

"I didn't know that I had to have a permit to open a salon." The man on the other end sighed now.

"If your salon has been open for more than five years, the health department didn't really know you existed. It's kind of recent; they implemented that rule in January of this year and there's been a lot of clean up in the wake of the new permits. There won't be any penalty, you just have to come down and fill out a form or two, then pay a small fee to get your paperwork in order." Lisa's face flooded with relief.

"That's it?" she asked him.

"That's it," he agreed.

"What about the paper products and stuff?"

"We normally do an inspection for those kinds of allegations; we want to see that kind of thing for ourselves."

"Well unless you come down right this very minute you're not going to find anything wrong; there's literally nothing left to find. We can't even operate like that."

"Can you prove that you were stocked up? Do you have any receipts for things that would show that you've bought supplies, or an inventory list?"

"I have all of that."

"Ok." He thought for a moment, and there was a bit of silence on the phone. "Get it all ready for me, and I'll make my inspection tomorrow. If you can show me that there was stock on the shelves then I'll pass you and get your permit ready."

"That sounds great." They hung up together and Lisa went into her office. Looking around, she almost called the Health

157

Department back, but decided to leave it alone. Camber thought she had had the upper hand, but in truth, Lisa did. Sure, she had taken the cleaning supplies and all of the paper towels and tissues, but she didn't have access to Lisa's office. In Lisa's office were two spare cases of Barbercide, an industrial carton of brown paper towels, and several boxes of hand tissues. She thought about putting them back on the shelves, but a devious thought leaked into her brain. The boxes had a thin layer of dust on them, which meant that they hadn't been moved – she had been buying supplies and had moved those in there when Damien worked out of her stock closet. Lisa pulled out receipts showing purchases from just two days before and got them ready to show the inspector. As it were, she paid her fee and passed inspection, but the problem was that Lisa still needed a hairdresser for her salon. The answer came in the form of a man named Corey. There was no ad in the paper yet – he simply walked in and asked for a job. Lisa obliged with an interview.

Lisa didn't recognize him, but during the interview, he kept smugly asking her if she remembered him. Lisa embarrassedly didn't. He was tall and had curly hair, and he had a large frame. When she looked at his application during the interview, the first giant red flag jumped out at her.

"You worked for Shear Madness?" Corey had the decency to blush.

"Yes, for a little while, but not now." Lisa ticked that off in her mind.

"Why not?"

"I'm having trouble with him; he screams at his employees, he doesn't pay us. I'm sick of it." Lisa didn't hesitate to call out the discrepancies. The last thing she wanted was that ugly creep back in her *salon.* She almost giggled when she thought about how snooty she sounded in her head.

"So you don't work for him but you're having trouble getting paid and being screamed at? Are you still there?" Corey shook his head.

"No, I left. I don't work there anymore. He tried to get me to sign a statement that I wouldn't work anywhere in ten miles of him after I left, but I said no."

"How long did you work there?"

"I've worked for him for quite a while. Matter of fact, I worked for him when Vinny did." Lisa snapped to attention and her memory swam. She slapped her hand down on her desk.

"You know what? I DO remember you! You look really great!" Lisa knew now why she didn't recognize him – this Corey was two hundred pounds lighter than he was when she had seen him last. He smiled.

"Thank you, I've been a diet for a while now, and I feel so much better." He said it with pride and Lisa could tell that he'd worked for it. She smiled back and continued.

"So what exactly are you looking for?"

"Well, I'm looking for a shop that has sub-contracting versus a wage. King is…well he's Colton King, and you're lucky if you get paid anything from him." Lisa knew what he meant.

"I'm actually open to both. My accountant says that I can go either way and pay a commission and a wage, or just a wage, or rent out a chair space permanently if I so choose to. I usually pay commission and let the chair go for a monthly price. I suppose it depends on the situation."

"I'd like to rent a chair, if it's possible." Lisa liked this idea. People who used her chairs and got paid commission were valuable.

"Sure, the cost to rent a chair is six hundred a month, and that includes full use of the salon and its supplies, your own cubby space that you can leave your stuff in, and access to all of your own clients."

"Six hundred dollars?" he asked incredulously. "Man, I can really only afford one hundred and fifty!" Lisa accidently laughed, and Corey looked dejected. She quickly regained her composure and tried not to feel insulted by his low balled offer.

"$150 doesn't even cover my light bill, and plus you have full access to the supplies in my shop. I'm not going to just give a chair space away." She said it patiently as if talking to a small child. Corey was still pouting.

"I understand, but gosh, that's awfully high. I'm just starting out!" Lisa sighed. She knew what he was talking about firsthand – she remembered sitting in her apartment cutting up her credit cards one by one and throwing them in the trash.

"Tell you what," she conceded. "I'll give it to you for half. Three hundred will get you in." Corey perked up.

"Deal," he said. They drew up paperwork and Corey left that afternoon with a spring in his step. Lisa had a full salon, all of her papers were in order, and there were customers to be cut. If she could glimpse into the future, she would have never hired him. She had no crystal ball though, so she continued blithely on. Corey asked if he could start closing the shop at night, and keep the salon open just a bit later than Lisa did. Lisa liked the idea of later clients, and agreed to do so, even adding another person to the schedule late so that they could take random clients that walked in. She closed with him a few times, and then was comfortable leaving him on his own. His rapport with his clients was excellent.

Corey loved women, but he was not necessarily a womanizer. He treated every woman like a princess, and his compliments sounded genuine, not phony or over-flattering. He would sit them in his chair, chat them up, and then give then excellent haircuts, all the while telling them how beautiful they were. He reminded Lisa briefly, of Vincenzo, but Vincenzo was often discriminatory, whereas Corey would talk to them all: short, fat, tall, and thin. Men were often impressed with their haircuts and tipped well. Lisa was under the impression that he was a really nice guy, and then she started to hear tales about his family.

"They're awful," Corey said, looking rejected. "My mother steals money from her job, and my father doesn't even try and stop her. He just shakes his head. Of course, I could see why he wouldn't care; he hasn't cared about anything for a really long time. My brother James got locked in an institution a while back and neither one of them even went to see him. When he got out they moved him in and so now they're all over there." Lisa knew that there were a lot of terrible things that could happen to a person, and she had no reason to believe that he was telling anything but the truth.

It didn't take long for things to go south, however. Since

Connecticut was already participating in winter, Lisa had brought out the space heater in her office for the bathroom, and turned on the heat for the salon. She expected that Corey would have turned off the heater at night, and turned down the central unit, but he did neither of those things. Lisa didn't hesitate to mention it.

"Remember when I said that $150 didn't cover my light bill? That wasn't really a joke. I need you to turn the lights and heaters off when you leave."

"I'm sorry; I'll try and remember next time." *He'd better*, she thought to herself. He was already cut enough slack on the chair. Lisa shook her head out and Kyle pulled up in front of the shop on his bicycle, shirt in hand as usual. When he opened the door, a gust of cold wind forced the door back and the glass shattered against the outside wall of the salon. Lisa groaned and reached for the phone, while Kyle dropped his shirt and went straight for the broom. She had two men there to fix the glass in a matter of hours. When Anne walked in for the usual wash and cut, she grimaced at Lisa.

"What happened?!" she asked, sitting down in the chair and putting her bag on the floor.

"Kyle broke the door," she said teasingly, winking at Kyle as he went into the bathroom.

"Did not, Lisa did it," he said, closing the door behind him. Anne chuckled. Lisa smiled.

"Nah, the wind caught it when he was coming in and it shattered."

"Likely excuse!" was a muffled reply from behind the door. Lisa and Anne laughed.

Lisa was also happy about other news. "Some good news for me," Lisa stated.

"What's that?"

"Alejandra is coming back in a month."

"Wow! Did she call you?"

"Yes, she called and said that her dad was getting better and that her mom was getting antsy, so she's coming back to the states."

"Great!" The haircut wore on, and the two women chatted

161

amicably. The men came to fix the door and it was finished before the end of the day. Corey stayed on and left the salon open for his extra hour. Kyle cleaned up and hopped on his bike to leave. Lisa left, too, but was disappointed when she came in the next day. Not only were the heaters on, but the lights were on too. Lisa called Corey at home.

"You left the lights on, Corey."

"Sorry," he said. It didn't ring true to Lisa so she continued.

"Look if you want to leave the lights on, you can pay six hundred for the chair. I told you I couldn't afford for you to drain the electricity and you're showing me disrespect after I did you a favor."

"I said I was sorry."

"Right." She hung up on him without answering. There was nothing more to be said, but she wouldn't be renting to him for much longer if this was how she was going to be treated. As she pulled into the driveway of the salon, her cell phone went off. It was Anne.

"Hey, how are ya?"

"I'm great. Listen, are you really ready for this thing? I'm not sure that we're ready."

"For what? The cut-a-thon?"

"Yes."

"Of course I'm ready. And so are you. It is twelve weeks away, there's nothing left now but the waiting. You've called the New Canaan Advertiser, they are going to run a story next month, you've printed up flyers that we're going to pass around town before the event."

"I know, but I mean, do you think that-"

"Stop it, now is not the time to get cold feet. It's fine. You've got everything planned out to the letter, don't you?"

"I'm so lucky I have you, Lisa."

"I know you are, your hair would be a mess." Anne giggled and hung up with Lisa. Lisa went into her office and grabbed the inventory sheets and started to count. She noticed that there were a few things missing – not on the grand scale as when Camber had left, but still here and there a couple of boxes of new combs or some bleach was gone, that kind of thing. Lisa felt a prickle in the back of her neck. When she finished the inventory, she went over to the bubble gum machine that she had installed shortly before Joan came. She emptied it every Friday and today was no exception, except there was no money in it. She sniffed. She had watched people buy gum out of it all week, there had to be something in it. There was nothing but gum. Lisa shook her head and looked around. Corey had to be doing something wrong, but she couldn't put her finger on anything. She did her best to push it out of her mind and went on back to work.

Kyle came in that afternoon, and business slowed down. He paced nervously and wrung his hands. When Corey walked through the front door, Kyle asked if he could go get a cup of coffee. Lisa told him to bring her one too, and Kyle left. Corey immediately started in.

"You know, I think he's got a problem."

"With who?" Corey didn't realize that he himself was going to have a problem.

"Not who, but what. I think he's got a drug issue," Corey said, waving his pinky finger and putting it to the side of his nose.

"You think he's on cocaine?" She had seen how Ashley and Gabriella acted while they were high and it wasn't the same.

"It has to be something. Look at him. He can't sit still." Lisa scoffed. She didn't believe Corey's accusations any more than she believed his apologies. In fact, the more she got to know him, the less she liked him. However, he did have a point. Kyle was always antsy, and sometimes his hands shook badly. He could solve that problem though – he would drink a cup of coffee or an energy drink and he would be ok. She countered Corey's accusations.

"He drinks like a gallon of coffee. And he's a great barber. In three months, I have had zero complaints from the men that come in. He does nice things for the shop too, like he puts out potpourri and rose petals and stuff like that. It's nice, and I like it."

"Still." Lisa looked at him sideways.

"Hey, did you empty out the bubblegum machine?" she asked him.

"What? No, why. Is it empty?" he asked her innocently.

"Yes. I usually empty it every Friday and I've been watching people put money in it all week but mysteriously, there's nothing in there." Corey didn't blink an eye.

"Well, I saw those two construction men over there messing around with it yesterday." Lisa couldn't deny it. The men that had come to fix the door had needed to move it so that they could hang the glass. She knew that they hadn't taken any money out though. Corey continued on.

"Anyhow, yea, I think if there's something missing, you should think about the one who has the problem." He nodded towards the door again, where Kyle was approaching the salon with their coffee.

"He doesn't have one," she hissed at him quickly. She walked over and let Kyle in. He handed her the coffee and she never had a chance to sugar it up and drink it – four clients walked in back to back, and they were busy for the rest of the day. Lisa left that afternoon to go pick up Joey from daycare and drop him off at her mother's while she grabbed a sandwich and drank her cold coffee. Time passed and the next time she looked up at her calendar, there wasn't even any snow on the ground. Winter, for all it had been worth, was coming to a close.

CHAPTER 17:
COUNTDOWN

March was definitely a hustle season for Lisa – not that it was particularly busy, but because Anne's fundraiser was finally  approaching. Things had of course, changed around the shop as they always did. Alejandra had come back from Columbia and had her spot in the salon. She had agreed to cut hair for Lisa and Anne at the Cut-a-thon and she had promised to bring some of her own people in. Corey was still plugging along, and although he had stopped leaving the heat on at night, it was because it was getting warm enough to leave them off altogether. She had raised the rent on his chair and he wasn't happy about that. Kyle was still around – biking in every day from the train and putting on his pressed shirts when he arrived. Lisa's mother helped around the shop when she could and Lisa ran things as smoothly as she could. Anne was caught up in a whirlwind of phone calls and plans, court cases of her clients and court dates of her own. The most interesting change in the weather was a call that she received one Friday afternoon about three weeks before the SPED*NET New Canaan event.

"Lisa's Classic Cuts, Lisa speaking." It always felt so good when she said that to whoever called.

"Lisa." The male voice on the other end sounded soft and unassuming. Still. "Lisa it's me."

"Hi Gene," she said blithely. "How are things?"

"Awful." He said it quietly, and with a fair amount of

humiliation in his voice. Gene was often soft spoken; he was a gentle giant, and although the children were afraid of him, they didn't know what they were missing. Lisa knew something was wrong.

"Tell me." It wasn't a question, but a simple request. She and Gene had gotten along like this for years. He obliged.

"I hate it here," he admitted. "The woman is unstable, and jealous, and really really jealous. And I mean, she loves me, don't get me wrong, but I'm not sure if it's less than an obsession, ya know? I can't leave the house without her – that was an exaggeration on her part too, she lives in a trailer park. She starts arguments; she tries to hit me when she gets angry. She thinks I'm dating other women, and she's doing all this other crap that just drives me to drink. She thinks I'm dating other people, Lisa! I don't even leave the house but to go to work and come back. She called me pathetic and a drug addict because I take so many medications for my back. She's flat out mean, Lisa, and I'm just sick of it."

"Wow…Gene you drove all the way out there for all of that? I wish someone would see the real you." Lisa was upset on his behalf.

"Well, I'm thinking about driving all the way back over there for my sanity."

"So, come."

"Can I still work in the salon?" Lisa smiled, and absently patted the back of her head.

"Sure, just don't offer me any more color jobs," she joked with him. He laughed for the first time since she had picked up the phone.

"I promise."

"I'll be there in a week." They hung up the phone together and Gene was at Lisa's salon in three days. She hugged him hard.

"That didn't take long." He smiled at her and picked her up off the floor in another bear hug.

"I already had my stuff in the car. I just wanted to see if I could come back to work." He stood her up on her feet and they chatted more while Lisa swept the floor. Kyle pulled up on his bicycle as usual, and pulled his pressed shirt off of the hanger that he always carried. Walking in the door, he greeted Lisa and Gene with smiles and jumped right in. All seemed well that day, and it was no surprise that Lisa was in high spirits when Anne came in.

"Hey lady," she said to Anne. Anne's mouth was pinched at the sides and her brow was creased with lines. She didn't reply, only looking at Lisa. Lisa crooked her finger at Anne and held the door open to her office. Anne went in without a word. When she got inside, she flopped down in the chair as if she carried a thousand pounds with her. Lisa raised an eyebrow.

"Arnie hasn't paid the mortgage in fifteen months and they're going to foreclose." Lisa's mouth fell open.

"What?! What do you mean they're going to foreclose? Can they even do that?"

"Yes, of course they can. I didn't know that the mortgage wasn't being paid. There were letters coming from the court addressed to me but he hid them before I came home. If you don't pay your mortgage, they can take your house." Lisa knew that much.

"What are you going to do?" Lisa cried.

"I've talked to some people and I can stall the foreclosure and insist on mediation. If I can stretch out the process, then I might be able to get it refinanced." Lisa shook her head, and reached into her purse. She pulled out her checkbook.

"Let me give you a loan." Anne protested.

"No, absolutely not. It's not that important." Of course it was.

"Yes, it is. Grabbing a pen from the cup by her computer, she flipped the top of the checkbook open and looked at her finances. Anne scooped the pen out of Lisa's hand and threw it over her shoulder.

"No."

"Yes!" Lisa picked up another pen and scribbled on a scrap of paper to make it work. Anne took that one too and threw it over her other shoulder. Then she picked up the cup that sat on the desk and held it above her head. Lisa grinned and shook her head. She dumped the checkbook back in her purse and fixed Anne with a level stare. Anne held up her hand.

167

"I'm going to try and fight the foreclosure. A couple nights ago I went to a meeting in Bridgeport. It was a questionable neighborhood and I felt out of place because I was the only white person in the group. There were some attorneys there that do foreclosure work. They gave a presentation about what to do to save your house from foreclosure. There were a lot of handouts from HUD (Department of Housing and Urban Development). It was so hot at this community center that the lawyers took off their jackets and rolled up their sleeves. Some counselor brought in boxes of donuts and large bottles of soda and water. A cheap, dusty, but big fan was pointing at us. The experience was unforgettable and it restored my faith in humanity. These lawyers were hot and sweaty and let's face it, no one in that group could afford to hire them. They were big shots by day and trying to help the man on the street by night. I myself am very guilty of routinely giving free talks to parents of children with disabilities. I spend countless hours talking to families that cannot afford lawyers. I see now that I am by no means the only person giving away services. I feel hopeful that there is something I can do. But if I can't save my home I'll go down in a dignified manner. I'll be alright. Really, I will be fine." Lisa eyed her suspiciously.

"Are you sure? Do you need anything? Can I buy some groceries? Clean your house? Anything?" Anne smiled and patted her hair.

"I could use a free haircut."

"Don't push it." They laughed together and Lisa took her hand and led her out to the salon floor and into the chair. She threw the smock on Anne. Anne tried to get up but Lisa pressed a hand to her shoulder.

"I actually didn't come for a cut, I came to give you fliers but I got the call about the house on the way here," said Anne.

"Well, it's on the house, so take it if you have time." Anne shrugged and sat back.

"I was just kidding about the free haircut," Anne told her. Gene leaned over and whispered conspiratorially to her.

"She usually doesn't take no for an answer." Lisa laughed and Anne smiled.

"So I learned," she agreed. Lisa was still smiling when Anne left. The salon got busy and they all went to work, with Gene and Lisa tag teaming customers with washing and drying. They had to – Gene couldn't stand still for very long, and the average haircut was long enough, but it wasn't exactly as though he had to stand still, but washing, drying, and then cutting could be difficult. Plus Lisa didn't want Gene to lose track of time, so they worked together to overcome obstacles. When it slowed down, Lisa went into her office to catch up on some paperwork, but after a while, Gene came in to complain.

"It's awfully slow," he started.

"It's the season," she said knowingly. During the weeks of March and April, it was a bit on the slow side.

"You should have told me." Didn't he already know? Lisa didn't say that. He huffed and was a bit miffed but soon his sunny self returned naturally and he went about his business. As he went into the store room, he came out again quickly, looking harassed and confused.

"Hey boss, I thought there was another box of combs in here." Gene jogged from one foot to the other, and she could tell he was agitated.

"There are, they are right there on the shelf in their place."

"Well, I looked."

"And?"

"Nothing."

"Nothing?" Gene shook his head and Lisa rolled her eyes. She followed Gene into the stock room who was standing in the place where the combs should have been. Sure enough, her last box of unused combs was gone. She shrugged it off, thinking that perhaps she had just lapsed and not ordered more. When Alejandra came in that afternoon, she asked about it; not because she thought Alejandra was stealing, but because Alejandra was loyal and if she had seen anything, she would tell Lisa. Unfortunately, she shook her head too.

"No, I haven't seen anything, but I think that man is stealing." Alejandra said in her thick Columbian way. Too bad there were three men that worked in the salon.

169

"Gene?" No way. Lisa knew better.

"No, no," she said waving her hand. "The other big one."

"Corey?" Alejandra snapped her fingers.

"That's the one," she said wisely. "I sometimes see him sniffing around and then watching me to see if I'm looking. I turn around he's pulling his hands out of his pockets or moving things around in his station. I can't be sure, I never see him clearly. But he's always looking for me. Sure sign of a thief." Alejandra knew that without hard evidence, there wasn't anything that Lisa could do. Corey rented his chair – he technically didn't work for Lisa, he just rented. The cost of his chair didn't cover his supplies and Lisa didn't provide what he needed for that exact reason. Alejandra and Lisa shook their heads together and looked at one another. What could they do?

When Lisa approached Corey, he again blamed someone else, this time the cleaning crew. Kyle just shook his head. Gene had nothing to say about the ordeal, but instead had his own problems. He was talking about opening a competing salon. Lisa felt the heat rising in her face.

"You're going to open a salon?" she asked him, quite sarcastically.

"No, I said I was *thinking* of opening a salon. I didn't say I was going to."

"Technical foul," Lisa said, putting her hands together to form a "t." "Where do you think you're going to open it?"

"Well, there's a salon for sale in Wilton that I was interested in." Lisa almost sighed with relief, but didn't want to be rude to her old friend.

"Oh, Wilton." Gene smiled at her.

"Yes, Wilton. You didn't think I would stomp your turf in New Canaan, did you?"

"Well, I..." she trailed off and he pointed at her in surprise.

"You did!" he told her. She held her hands open and he smiled at her.

"Well, the reason I'm even thinking about it is because I saw that there's a salon for sale in Wilton in an ad on Craigslist." Lisa's brow wrinkled. The internet was in full swing now, and Craigslist was a website that you could buy and sell your wares on, offer free services and just about anything under the sun that you could think of. She didn't get to the computer much and while she knew how to use it, she was much better at cutting hair. She was interested in the salon, though.

"Oh, ok, now you're starting to make sense. Do you know how much it is?"

"Not yet, but I know that she's selling off pieces of equipment and stuff online too, so if we check it out and we don't like it, there still might be something that you might find." Lisa was nervous and her next question was obvious.

"How are you going to pay for it, anyhow?"

"Well that's why I'm bringing it up to you. I thought we could go half, if the price is reasonable." That got her gears going. She knew from experience that it wouldn't take long for the salon to pay for itself, especially if she only had to plunk down half of the initial costs to start up.

"Call her and make an appointment to see her, and we'll drive up and check it out." Gene made the arrangements for the next week and she got her finances in order and put together a packet for the bank in case she needed a loan. When the next week rolled around, she scheduled Alejandra and Kyle to work the salon and had her mother come and open while Joey was in day care. When Gene picked her up, Lisa couldn't hold her surprise at who the passenger was.

"Hi, Susan," she said to Gene's mother, who sat primly in the front and made no signs of getting out. Lisa slid into the back seat and closed the door behind her. Gene grinned at Lisa.

"This here is my right hand woman when it comes to all of my business deals." The old woman smiled.

"Yes, I think it's a wise thing that Gene brought me along. You just can't trust some people," she said pointedly. Lisa sat back and tried to ignore the statement. Susan was the master of the backhanded compliment and the directly veiled insult. Lisa had no idea why Gene had brought her along – she wasn't a hairdresser and didn't have the foggiest clue as what to look for. But Gene was Gene and she accepted that. He would always be under his mother's thumb and despite his settlements and his job, Lisa suspected the real reason she had come along was because she was privately funding his effort in the matter. She still didn't want to be a business partner with her. They arrived at the salon without a hitch, and a woman waited to greet them outside. She introduced herself as Carol.

The woman was a robust forty or so, with bright eyes and of course, perfect hair. Her shop was called Scissor's Palace. The salon was very nice, and had seven chairs, plus space for one more. It looked like there had been a chair there recently that had been taken out. The countertops were faux marble and the waiting area was walled off into a comfortable and roomy sitting room with chintz armchairs that matched the décor of red and gold. There was a double restroom and there was one door marked employees only that Lisa found out led into an employee break room, a giant store room for supplies, and an office where the woman conducted her daily business. It was beautiful and Lisa was almost convinced. Susan caught her eye and nodded. Gene looked beside himself. Susan stepped forward.

"How much for the whole kit and caboodle?" Susan didn't miss a beat, but without looking at the woman, inspected her fingernails, feigning disinterest.

"I'm asking seventy thousand for everything." Susan snapped to.

"Now I understand that you've got quite a place here, but that's a bit much, don't you think? The chairs are worth 5 a piece and that's 35 grand, but the building's lease doesn't cost that much. The furniture is in good condition but it isn't new. How do you justify that amount? The whole thing should be less than 60." Lisa suddenly knew why Gene had brought her. Susan was nothing if not a critical thinker. The woman looked around at her salon.

"I have no choice." Lisa stepped in with her own questions. Gene looked like he was watching a tennis match.

"This is a beautiful shop, why would you sell it anyway? Surely it's making money?" Carol took her time in answering. When she did, Lisa noticed a note of sadness in her voice.

"Yes, it's made money. It has been a good salon. Last year,

172

however, I had an employee that decided to steal everything that I had and it cost me thousands to take care of it."

"Oh god," Lisa said, appalled. "What happened?"

"Well the man and his wife both worked here for me and it seemed ok. I had made him an assistant manager and given him access to the salon's account so that he could order stock and take care of things when I was gone, which at the time I was gone a lot because I was trying to open another salon in Westport. He didn't pay the lease, he returned supplies and kept the cash from the account and covered the books. Corey and his wife siphoned 20 grand off the account in three months and he disappeared one afternoon with thousands of dollars' worth of equipment, supplies, and anything else that wasn't nailed down. I fired them both, and I almost pressed charges but instead I decided to sue him for damages." Lisa's stomach started to churn.

"What did you say their names were?"

"Corey and Nancy Latbatt." Lisa thought she might throw up.

"I know him," she said quietly. Gene looked at her knowingly and frowned.

"Well, I made the stipulation that he couldn't work in Wilton anymore, him or his wife. It was in the court order. The only problem is now I have to clean up the mess that he made."

"So you're selling your salon." Susan chimed in bluntly. The other woman nodded. Lisa felt bad for her, because it was just too much. Lisa made a mental note to start watching Corey like a hawk, and to charge a higher price on his chair in hopes that he would leave. She would prosecute him if he tried to do the same thing that he had done to this poor woman. She shook her head.

"Carol, I love your salon. I do. But we just can't afford it," Lisa said sadly. Carol nodded.

"I understand. I normally wouldn't charge so much, but like I said..." she trailed off. Susan finished.

"Well, you've got a hell of a mess to clean up, sounds like." Lisa nodded, feeling sorry for Carol. They shook hands and the three talked the entire way home about the salon they had visited. Gene dropped her off at the salon and Lisa went into her office and thought heavily about what came next. Should she fire him?

173

Should she install a camera? She didn't have to, because three weeks later, he was gone again like a thief in the night, with all of his supplies and all of his gear from his personal station. She opened her shop to find the air condition running at full blast and the floor not swept. The cleaning crew didn't come in on the night before, so Lisa swallowed it all. When she opened her office door, there was a note telling Lisa that he was quitting because his wife needed help at home with their three year old twins. He didn't take everything that wasn't his – just what he could use or carry. Lisa sighed, and looked at the calendar. She didn't have time to hire anyone else right at the moment – the cut-a-thon was in two more weekends. In fact, she needed to call everyone again and make sure that all the hairdressers she had chosen would do their part.

In the meantime, Anne passed out fliers and posted them in every window. It was looking good so far, and many people that weren't going to attend had already pledged. As she wore down each day, Anne made a little progress, and as Lisa closed the shop, she got a little farther too. It was like they were a cog and a wheel that fit so perfectly together but still operated separately. It was a handsome relationship and both women managed to thrive.

CHAPTER 18:
THE CUT-A-THON

The weeks had passed and it was finally the day of the cut-a-thon. Lisa showed up with Alejandra at 9am. They both had a tray of cookies that Lisa had offered up for sale; Lisa and her mother had stayed up baking. The event would start in an hour. The weather was on their side; the sun was shining and it was about seventy or so. A table was set up for donations and tips. Another long buffet table was set up behind them to hold their essentials

and then it was all business from there. Alejandra and Lisa found Anne.

"Looks good," Alejandra said to Anne, nodding her approval.

"Thanks," said Anne breathlessly. "Did you call the other barbers?" she asked Lisa.

"Yes, but not all of them are coming." Lisa smiled.

"That's fine!" Anne chirped. They climbed the platform and laid their stuff out respectively. Kyle came next and then Gene showed up behind him. Two of the haircutters that Lisa had recruited from The Yankee Clipper Barbershop came together. Joan had volunteered to take time away from her flowers and was followed by Chi, who had also agreed to come. They took their places and the cut-a-thon began. Lisa cut hair for three hours straight, and the fundraiser had already made three hundred dollars by her alone. The rest of the festival was running nicely, and Anne came up to Lisa, who was taking a break from cutting. Another hairdresser had replaced her and was standing behind a client talking to him.

"Hey, wanna sit for a while?" she asked Lisa. "I've got to

watch the cash and tips for this part of the fundraiser."

"Sure, I could use a long break. How are things going?"

"Great, everything is going smoothly."

"Watch the cashbox for me; I'm going to grab some food." She left Lisa in front of the box, which was filling up quickly. The tip jar was getting fat too, and it wasn't long before Anne was back with two hotdogs and two sodas for the pair of them. They ate together and Lisa started to get up. Anne put a hand on her shoulder.

"Stay with me," she invited. "I need someone to help me watch the cash." Lisa needed to take a quick break but came back quickly. When she got back over to Anne, Anne was staring at Kyle with a furrowed brow.

"What's wrong?" she asked.

"I think Kyle is pocketing tip money." Lisa groaned inwardly.

"How do you know?"

"Well, I've been watching him put his hand in the jar as if he's putting money in but I think I saw him take money back out once, and I'm almost positive that I just saw him put his hand in his pocket after a client tipped him."

"Seriously?"

"Yes."

"Ok, keep an eye on him and we'll see how it goes." And they did, not learning any more than they had known before they started watching. One thing was clear – either they were completely wrong about him stealing or he was better than either of them thought. Joan came down to the table and sat with them for a few minutes, eating a hot dog and drinking lemonade.

"This is great," she commented.

"It's because it's the real thing," Anne said. "It's organic, freshly squeezed and made right before we got here." Joan looked impressed and raised her cup.

"Great stuff." She finished her meal and went back to the stand. Lisa sighed.

"I guess I'd better go cut some hair too," she said. Anne nodded this time and let her go.

The day wore on and Lisa approached Anne. "Hey kiddo!"

Lisa said brightly. "Are you going to get your hair cut?"

"No way!" she chirped. Lisa laughed and Anne slung an arm around her shoulders. Robbie and Erik weren't far behind; they were walking together up to the group while Ieva had run ahead. She was far from the young girl that had come into Lisa's shop for the first time almost nine years earlier. She was, in fact, a young woman. Her shyness was limited to total strangers and sometimes large crowds, but here she was in her element – many of the people that had turned out were part of the special needs community, and here it was that she could bask in the glory of her friends without fear. She tugged on Anne's arm.

"Mom, I need more lemonade." Robbie and Erik were laughing and Lisa waved her hand off. She could watch the cash box while Anne and the kids headed to the lemonade station. The happy family went and Lisa sat watching. She observed Kyle for a while and Alejandra, who was about to take a break. Joan had long gone – her condition was catching up with her. The afternoon wore on and the sun shone brightly. An hour later, Anne came back to Lisa with her kids and they all sat together at the table where the cashbox sat. The tip jar behind the barbers was as empty as ever, with only a few dollars in it. Lisa's heart sank when she thought about it; she would have to pay that back.

The crowd started to thin out and Anne decided that it was time to close everything down. She took Ieva with her and Robbie and Erik stayed with Lisa while Lisa and Alejandra collected their things. The other barbers were packing as well, and the chairs that were empty were being folded away by some of the staff that had come to help Anne set up. Lisa took the money from the cashbox and put it in the envelope that Anne had given her. Then she went to the tip jar and pulled out the handful of cash that was in there. She counted it, disappointed. There was less than fifty dollars. She went over to the table where the hairdressers were packing up.

"I know," she said loudly, "That there was at least fifty to a hundred dollars in this container. Would someone like to explain to me where it went?" Gene raised his eyebrows and pulled two dollars out of his pocket and handed it to Lisa.

"That's all I've got, you can have it," he told her. She put it with the other money.

"I thought this was for charity? That's terrible," Lisa said. Alejandra shook her head and glanced at Kyle.

"I put my tips in the jar," she said matter of factly. "Maybe someone took the money." Kyle was bending over putting things away in a box. When he straightened up, Lisa was looking him in the face.

"Sorry you didn't make as much as you could have," he said smartly. Lisa wanted to smack him, but refrained. He wasn't going to admit anything.

When Anne came, Lisa pulled her off to the side.

"There was 37 dollars in the tip jar. I know there was more than that to start with because I was handed at least fifty dollars in tips myself.

"What do you think?"

"I think you were right." Anne and Lisa looked at each other. They spoke at the same time.

"I can pay it all back," said Lisa.

"Don't worry about it," said Anne at the same time.

"No, I invited him to work today." Lisa could feel the top of her head getting hot, which was not a good sign.

"It's ok."

"It's your fundraiser! It's for charity!"

"It's ok, really." Anne knew that Lisa couldn't control what other people did – especially while her back was turned. It wasn't anyone's fault except Kyle's. They bickered for a few more moments and Anne held up her hand.

"Stop. Just hang on a second." She walked away and came back with a gentleman who had had his haircut by Alejandra earlier. She could tell that pretty Columbian had cut his hair – his sideburns were cut practically to his eyebrows, something that Alejandra was famous for. Anne introduced him to Lisa as Ray.

"Lisa, Ray plays a big part in SPED*NET New Canaan and I think that you should talk to him." Lisa turned red in the face and Ray grabbed her hand.

"I understand that you've had a problem with the tip jar over here?" he said quietly to her. Lisa stammered but couldn't speak.

"Lisa," he told her. "I understand where you're coming from. It's hell when you feel responsible for something that someone else has done. But look at the bigger picture." He put his arm around her shoulder and she felt comforted. He waved his other hand out in a span before them at the sky. "Your barbers and your friends brought in almost three grand today. That's three grand that will go towards a sensory friendly park or maybe a boundless playground. We have three thousand." She felt warm, and didn't know why. She was still in the wrong.

"I still want to pay it back."

"Then volunteer again. Pay it forward. We achieved our goal today." Lisa's eyes teared up and he hugged her. "It's ok. Really." Lisa caught Anne's eye and she nodded approvingly. Lisa hugged him back and they talked for a few more minutes; then Ray was gone.

"How did he do that?" Lisa asked Anne.

"Do what?" He made me feel good about that whole situation.

"He's like that, he does it a lot."

"He's nice. What does he do for a living? He must be a counselor. He's great!"

"Actually, he's a car salesman." Lisa laughed.

"You're kidding."

"Nope. We met because his eight year old daughter autism. She and Ieva go to the same therapist." Lisa shook her head. You never could tell. Alejandra came over to join the two and pulled them away from everyone else.

"Kyle is bragging about how much money he has in his pocket. He's talking about going out for a steak dinner and tipping the waitress with a fifty." Alejandra had her lip curled up in disgust. "I know what he did." She said it to Lisa, and Lisa nodded.

"I can't prove it, Alejandra." Alejandra shook her head and turned around.

"You can send him home." She said it as she was walking away, and to Lisa, it didn't sound like a bad idea. She went over to Kyle and told him that he could leave his things and she would get them and take them to the shop. He liked the sound of it and told her that he needed a cup of coffee. He got on his bike and left them there. Ray had said that she didn't have to pay it back, but she would figure out something.

The sun was setting and everyone was gone – it was just Lisa, Anne and the cleanup crew now, and Alejandra. The kids had gone back with Anne's nanny, who Lisa had met and liked very much. It had been a good day. As Lisa and Alejandra were pulling away, Anne started to cry in earnest and had to pull over to the side of the road.

CHAPTER 19:
THE DEATH OF A BARBER

Lisa pulled into Hoyt's Funeral Home with tears in her eyes before the service even started. She had known Orv for a long time, and he had given her the first job she had ever had. The day of the cut-a-thon had proved to be too much for Orv, and his collapse that day had proved fatal. She had called Orv's home number and spoken to his wife about it - to check on him. Phyllis had filled her in on Orv's critical condition.

It seemed that Orv had been sicker than he was letting on about – or perhaps than he was willing to admit. It was no secret that Orv was old. Hell, he was old when Lisa had met him fourteen years ago as a wet behind the ears stylist straight out of hairdressing school. When they were working together he would often thump his chest with a fist and brag that he had already had three separate bypass surgeries and was still going strong. It was true but in the time that had passed he had a whopping six more surgeries on his heart.

The cough that had plagued him was part cold and part Marlboro, to hear Orv tell it. He had never given up his cigarettes and had a bit of a nicotine hack, but recently it was no ordinary smoker's cough. According to Dr. Ming in the emergency room, it was all pneumonia. Orv had been taking over the counter cold medicines for nearly a month without any kind of medical treatment, Phyllis had told Lisa. The combination of his illness, the self-medication, and the heart condition had left Orv in Intensive Care.

She had called Anne with the update but it wasn't until the following Friday that a man came in that Lisa didn't recognize and asked if she was the owner of the salon. Lisa had smiled and nodded, thinking nothing out of the ordinary. She thought he looked familiar, but couldn't place him. He took his hat off and wrung it in his hands. Then he dropped a bomb.

"Miss Lisa, you don't remember me?" She furrowed her brow.

"You look familiar but I…" Lisa shook her head and tried to remember. He was kind of short, and was working on a shaggy beard. His eyes were red rimmed and he looked a bit wrinkled, as though he slept in his clothes. The old man had rubbed his face in his hands and then down his shirt.

"I guess you wouldn't." Surprised tears ran down his face. "I guess you wouldn't know where a man in this town could get a hot shave, do you?" He wrung his hat in his hands until it was a twisted knot and stood there before Lisa in her salon, sobbing once and then gaining control. Then it hit Lisa: Jerry, a regular of Orv's barber shop.

Lisa didn't hesitate. She walked over to the door and flipped the sign over and locked the door. Then she walked over to a chair and patted it.

"Right here," she said. Jerry was a little fuzzy – it looked like he probably hadn't had a shave since Orv had gone into the hospital. She could feel tears welling up in her eyes but she knew that she wouldn't be able to shave him if she started now. Jerry didn't have to say anything to her, Lisa already knew the truth but she braced herself to hear the grim news anyhow. She invited the words.

"How is he?" He sat patiently in the chair waiting while she prepped towels and found a straight razor. She kept an old fashioned men's shaving kit in her desk for moments like this – it had in fact been a going away present from Orv himself when she had finally decided to make her move. It was his way of telling her that he was proud of her and reminding her to keep her roots. She had used it three times since and kept it tucked away neatly. Jerry remained silent until she came out with it.

"Gone." He said simply. He couldn't say anything else without breaking down into unmanly tears. "The old fart is gone." He shook his head and she smiled back at him. It was Orv's and Jerry's fondest insult. Lisa leaned him back in the chair.

"Wanna jaw about it?" she asked him. That was another one

of Orv's. Jerry picked it up.

"You bet your sweet bippy!" he said, and they laughed together. Together they felt a burning in their chests that said life would go on and Orv would be disappointed if they pined away for him. Together, these two comrades in grief refused to grieve and felt the strangeness of being happy while someone they'd loved had passed. Lisa learned a few things along the way.

"I've been getting a shave from Orv for thirty years," he told her. "He's actually my sister's brother in law. I came out of the military and settled here and I've been playing checkers outside of Jacobs barber shop since." Lisa hadn't known and was impressed.

"We were pretty close, I suppose. Did a few holidays together. Phyllis used to make some mean banana pudding." Lisa nodded appreciatively.

"Orv gave me my chance," she said.

"I remember! He told you that if you left him you wouldn't go nowhere. You haven't come back yet," he said chuckling. She shook her head and laughed.

"That just motivated me to prove him wrong."

"That's good, it's what he wanted."

"How so?"

"Orv talked so good about you when you worked there you'd think the sun shone out of your backside, lady. 'That gal is going to have two or three salons open if she keeps that up,' he would say. We'd hear a bit of news about you now and then; you know how word travels around town. He'd always say, 'See, I told you she would do something right.'" Lisa couldn't believe her ears. She hadn't ever considered that she would get bragged about – that wasn't too much like him so his compliments were gold.

"Really?!" she asked Jerry incredulously. Lisa stopped for a minute. "Then why in the hell did he give me such a hard time?"

"Cause he didn't want you to go, I guess." They had lapsed into thoughtful silence as she piled a hot towel on Jerry's face and he sat there with it cooling.

A sharp rap sounded and Lisa jumped, awakened from a trance. It was then she realized that she had been reveling in her memory; Lisa was sitting in her car with the engine running, but her mind had been with Jerry in the salon the day she had been told that Orv had passed away. Her eyes felt gritty and she realized that she had been crying the entire time. She looked out and there was Jerry, dressed in his best black suit knocking at her car window. She pulled the keys out of the ignition and threw them in her purse. He opened the door for her.

"You gonna sit in there all day?" he asked her. She smiled and shook her head, but didn't speak. She just didn't trust her voice. He offered his arm and she took it; they walked to the doors of Hoyt's together. The inside was beautiful, and people were milling about.

Hoyt's was a very nice place. The carpet was lush and deep blue; the walls were creamy white with nice flowers hanging here and there. The halls were wide and there were people milling about in their best black clothes. When Lisa got to the chapel of the funeral home, she saw that Orv had been placed in a beautiful chestnut casket with a blue lining. She didn't want to see him in the casket and tried not to look as Jerry led her down the aisle.

Monsignor Palin would be leading a service, speaking a bit and then the attendees would have a chance to share something. Then they would head down to the gravesite where they would pay their last respects. Monsignor Palin was already in his place at the front of the chapel at the funeral home, but what caught Lisa's attention is that the chapel was nearly full and they were bringing folding chairs in. Men were lining the walls while women sat. Jerry steered her towards the front by the arm, sitting close to Orv's family. She broke away as he sat and found Phyllis. They hugged as if they were long lost friends.

"Thank you for coming. I appreciate you calling the other night too," was all she said to Lisa. Lisa had called Phyllis after Jerry left and offered her help with anything she needed.

"I'm so sorry." Phyllis patted Lisa on the face with a liver spotted hand and turned silently to the next well-wisher. Lisa cleared her throat and people began taking their seats. Every pew in the chapel was full and each folding chair had someone in it. People still stood against the walls, and Lisa was amazed at the turn out. Monsignor Palin stepped up to the pulpit and began with the Lord's Prayer.

"We are here to remember the best barber in New Canaan. I started to get a haircut before I had the service but I didn't want to insult his memory." The crowd chuckled. Monsignor Palin was famous for making the services pleasant in the face of grief.

"Orv Byron was born and raised here in New Canaan. He married his wife in this town; he took over his father's business at the barber shop and cut hair for many years. He was a husband, a father, a brother and a son, not to mention one heck of a barber."

"There wasn't a man in New Canaan that Orv didn't know by name. Orv took over his father's shop when he was 25 and he made a name for himself that was as good as Jacob's. He could stand in front of the checkerboard and call you out from the street. He would tell you that you needed a haircut and then talk you into one whether you really needed it or not. He loved his wife and loved his business and knew New Canaan like the back of his hand." The man droned on, but Lisa's ears were buzzing and she was at the height of her senses. She could hear rustling in the back and the soft sobs of Phyllis in front of her. She could hear Jerry breathing next to her. Lisa felt canned, for a moment. Surely there was something poignant that someone could say about Orv that didn't seem like his life history or something that the monsignor would say for anyone else. As he closed his statements he invited people to come and speak. Lisa watched as people filed up to the podium and shared their loving memories. Phyllis was first. She shuffled up to the podium and Monsignor Palin helped her take the step up. She addressed them all.

"Who's cryin'? You'd better stop, Orv would be so disappointed. My husband wouldn't want anyone here to shed a single tear for him; in fact, he just might call you all a bunch of women." A deep rumble of laughter came from the old men. She continued.

"Orv was the stubbornest old man you'd ever meet, but he was well worth it. I'm here to tell you folks that life is short, too short to be standing up here a whole long time jawin' your ear off. The next time your friend calls, go out with them when they invite you, or take that day off and go with your family up the coast. You don't know what you're going to miss." She nodded her head

185

towards the open casket where Orv was made up like a wax doll. "I don't think he'd have wanted this thing open, but I chose to have it open because I wanted to make sure he was really gone. He was dang near impossible to kill – not that I haven't tried a couple of times in our life." She was on a roll. You could tell that she really loved her husband, and would miss him terribly – her bravado was something fierce though, and she was making jokes to mask her pain.

"My Orv was real big on living life just the way it was. 'Phyllis, relax,' he'd tell me. 'Things have a funny way of working themselves out,' was something that he was fond of saying," She shook her head sadly. "Turns out, he was right. Orv lived to be 85 doing whatever he wanted, and not worrying about a thing when I would be tearing my fool head off trying to fix the world's problems. I never did get that about him, but he would wave his hand at me and tell me that I was worried enough for both of us. I guess I won't have to do that anymore." She sobbed. "Look at me, fool that I am." She shook her head again and Monsignor Palin helped her off the stage. Lisa thought about getting up there but couldn't move. The last speaker came up and it was an old man in a yellow Hawaiian shirt. Lisa had noticed him earlier – no one else was dressed like that. As he approached the podium he stopped and hugged Phyllis, who had taken her seat.

"Orv gave me this shirt when he and Phyllis came back from Honolulu on their honeymoon. I had told him to bring back something ugly and he really rose to the occasion. I was kind of hoping for a woman." Everyone laughed. "I thought he could have it back, I hear its paradise where he's at." That was all he'd said, and he too made his way back down the step and to his seat. Monsignor Palin took the podium again and said a few closing words. It was time to go to the cemetery to lower Orv's casket into the ground. They filed out mechanically one by one and got into their cars. Lisa pulled out into the procession and followed the line to the cemetery gates. Everything was ready.

The pall bearers were gathered around the casket, pulling it from the back of the hearse. Andrew was there, looking much older than he had when she had last seen him, though the years had

186

been kind. He looked rather grim, however. She found Jerry and sat in a folding chair that had been provided. Some of the people from the funeral didn't come – they had gone on, and there were less people here. Lisa found herself sitting next to a familiar face. She smiled at her and didn't say anything. The funeral director said his prayers and lowered Orv Byron into his open grave. They prayed together, and the service was over. As the attendees milled about, she approached the woman that she had been sitting next to.

"Don't I know you?" she asked the woman. Of course she did, it was a rhetorical question.

"Nope, never seen you before in my life," said the other. They laughed and shook hands. Jerry excused himself for a cigarette and left the two. The woman was Eleanor Aquatne, the owner of the property that Orv's barber shop was sitting on.

"How's things going in the salon?" They turned away from the grave site and started walking towards where everyone was parked.

"Great. I'd have never gotten that place if it weren't for your digging. I'm still there; I've been there for quite a long time."

"Wow, so you're successful! Excellent! Have you thought about moving into a bigger salon?" This particular woman was quite a known name in real estate in New Canaan. She had several properties leased out and a few houses that she owned that were for sale. Orv's shop had been one of them.

"Well, I've thought about it, but I can't find anything that's right. I'm going to keep looking though; I think there's something out there for me." Lisa had thought about moving for a while – maybe even opening a new salon – but some days she didn't want to think about it. Some days she just wanted to cut hair. The lady waved a hand in the air.

"That's great. I don't know what I'm going to do with the property now that Orv's gone. He's been there so long it doesn't feel right for there to be anything else."

"Why don't you give it to Lisa," said a voice from behind them. It was Phyllis and Andrew, walking arm in arm. Phyllis had overheard their conversation. Lisa shook her head in alarm.

"Oh, no Phyllis, I couldn't do anything like that, I -" Phyllis cut her off.

"Sure you can. He's not going to use it any more. I think if anyone would love that place to pieces as much as he did, it would be you, wouldn't it? I think he would like the idea." Lisa stopped and looked at Phyllis.

"Really?"

"Sure, he always talked about the girl that he gave her big break to." Lisa rolled her eyes and smiled.

"We'll see," was all that she said. Eleanor looked at Lisa and they walked in silence for a few minutes. Phyllis and Andrew passed them and got into the funeral home's escort car and drove away. As they watched them leave, Eleanor spoke.

"You want to check it out? Couldn't hurt anything." Lisa shrugged and wrote her number down for the other woman. She was a little excited about the prospect of it. Who would have thought after all this time she would return to Orv's barber shop and move into where he had stood for so many years. When she met with Eleanor the next week, she could really see the toll that time had taken on things.

The place was pretty dusty around the edges, and Orv's office was a box stained with nicotine. The shop was clean and neat, but a crumbling window sill over here and a crack in the marble counter top over there made all of the difference. She could see the wall paper peeling down one corner of the wall and a bit of damage on the ceiling. Lisa could see much more than that, however, in her mind's eye.

In her memories, Lisa could see herself standing shoulder to shoulder with Orv, cutting hair and listening to old stories that he had told a hundred times. She could see the old TV that Orv had replaced when she worked there – the one that had gotten Ashley in so much trouble. Lisa ran her hand along the leather chairs and the counter tops that were in charge of holding all sorts of supplies. Eleanor said nothing, and Lisa went home that day with Eleanor's business card with a listing number on the back.

She weighed her options. The economy had not been kind to the landlord that owned her building, and her lease was teetering on the edge of extinction – after the announcement that he was raising her rent for the year. Lisa had already given up her home and moved into a tiny apartment to save money. Jacob's would need some touching up if she intended to move into it. Her profits were decent and they kept food on the table, but there was little to be said for retirement or college. The economy in the United States was becoming a hot boiled mess and Lisa wasn't sure if she wanted to put her bid in for a hefty loan to fix the place up.

No one ever did but it would still take her nearly six years and two other locations to say yes.

Lisa was sweeping up debris from the salon floor for the third time that day and she was getting worried. Her salon was due to open in 24 hours, and the final touches were being put on the insides of Jacob's Barber Shop. Things were going according to

plan, but her nerves were stretched raw.

She had finally decided that she wanted to move into Jacob's barber shop. Out of the blue she paid a visit to Eleanor and she was pleased to find out that no one had ever been interested in the barber shop even though that's what it had been

forever. Phyllis had given her blessing to move into Orv's space and so she went back to her roots. She thought, however that the place could use some modern touches. The walls had been scrubbed and all the cracks had been sealed. The floors had been refinished and the placed had had a good airing out. New Wainscot paneling was installed on the walls; the floor, the roof and the drywall ceiling had been replaced and painted.

Lisa had decided to install some new chairs and save the marble counter tops – they were so classic-looking and they made her feel at home. She decorated the place so that it still invited the old men, but welcomed women too. It was nice. She had even decided that she would keep the name "Jacob's Barber Shop" on the window and put "Lisa's Classic Cuts" underneath it instead of scraping it off. This was the current source of her ire. She had already told the decal installer that she didn't want the name removed and he was dabbing on the solution that would lift

Jacob's name right off the glass. She banged on the glass with an open palm and when he looked up, she made a slashing motion at her throat to make him stop. He shrugged and wiped it off. Then he began washing the window underneath so that he could apply the decal to it. She sighed.

Alejandra was there with her, moving boxes of supplies into a back room. She had broken into a sweat as she hauled boxes but shrugged off Gene's help. She had fired Kyle shortly after the SPED*NET New Canaan event – there was no way she was keeping him. Chi, who was still her Saturday girl, was due to come in that afternoon and help move things too, but she wasn't there yet. Anne came to see the commotion and fell in love with the new place.

"Oh god, it looks great in here!" she exclaimed. And it did – she had visited Jacob's a couple of times before the fundraiser to meet with Orv and make sure that he knew what to do and when to do it when the time came. It was almost ready, except for the sweeping and wiping down of the dust. Anne put her things down and pitched in immediately. When she and Lisa were taking a break, Lisa told her what was going on in her life, besides moving the salon, of course.

"I can't get Larry to pay his child support." Anne's face turned red with anger. She knew exactly how Lisa felt.

"Take him to court."

"I can't afford a lawyer." Anne slapped her hand down on the counter and gave Lisa a level stare.

"Seriously did you just say that to me right now? You can't afford a lawyer?" Anne was angry for Lisa. She was a good woman that worked hard and Larry fell into Arnie's grain of men that wouldn't keep up their child support. She hated it, and was glad that she had semi-solved her problems. She would, on the other hand help Lisa avoid the misery that she had endured.

"Anne, I can't run to you every time I need legal help!"

"Why not, I come here when I need a haircut." She patted her hair. "Which I'm due for." Lisa laughed at her and twiddled the handle of the broom.

"I don't know."

"Look, I tell you what, we'll trade. I'll help you wring Larry and you give me a month's worth of free cuts and colors." Lisa added it up in her head and realized that it would be about the cost of a retainer. She nodded.

"Alright then." Anne smiled and they changed the subject. She looked towards the corner of the room, where the barber pole had been taken down.

"Are you taking that out?" she asked Lisa.

"No! Oh, no, I just had it cleaned and serviced so that it looks spiffy. I would never take that down. I want to do things just the way Orv did: Come in, turn the sign over on the door and turn the pole on."

"I like it that you're kind of leaving it the way it is. I mean, I love the updates that you've made but I like that the concept kind of stays the same."

"I think it should. That pole meant a lot to a lot of people for a long time." They lapsed into silence, staring at the pole.

"I wonder why they're red and white," said Anne absently. Lisa glanced over and broke from the reverie.

"Well, barbers used to do more than just cut hair. Barbers were often dentists, surgeons and did bloodletting to try and cure people of certain kinds of disease. They would use white cloth bandages to clean and compress which of course need washing after they were used, and twisted and hung to be dry. They would make red and white stripes and that's how you could find him, because the cloths would hang outside. The first barber poles were made of wood and paint." Anne looked at Lisa agog.

"What?" she asked, surprised.

"How did you even know all of that?" Lisa chuckled. Gene, who had been quiet until now, spoke up.

"I made her Google it." Lisa rolled her eyes.

"I asked him to show me how to look up on the Internet where I could get my barber pole looked at because I didn't want it to get stuck when I first turned it on. I found out some interesting history, and also that this particular pole is an antique and is worth quite a bit."

"Neat. What about the one with the blue stripes?"

192

"America."

"Gotcha." The silence lapsed again and they wiped, swept and hefted in good time until the salon was almost completely moved and unpacked. The black leather chairs were polished to a shine and the chrome stands gleamed. The floor was new and it too was looking its best. The window man had long gone, and Lisa had given it a final once over. It was very handsome. When the place was cleaned and polished, and the others had filtered out, it was just her and Anne again in the salon. Lisa looked at her.

"Are you serious about the haircuts thing?"

"Absolutely. It really bothers me that you're not getting what is owed to you. You didn't make Joey alone, and if he can't find a way to support you while being there, he still needs to support Joey when he's *not* there." Anne had spent long nights in bed thinking the same things. She had pushed and pushed and pushed for her rights with Arnie – and in some ways was still lacking. She had managed to save her house, but she laid off all the nannies and put a tenant in the room they usually lived in. The boys had all been put to work; Robbie worked at the town pool while Karl performed magic tricks at birthday parties. Erik was babysitting. Ieva was grown now and battling Diabetes while Anne just tried to manage it all. Occasionally she failed, as all good women must, to know when she was about to break.

"Trust me," she told Lisa. "It can be done." It was Lisa's turn to reflect now. Anne really had done it – they had been entwined in each other's lives for a long time and Lisa had seen it with her own eyes. In truth, they were kindred spirit. Larry had been gone a while and while he didn't leave her floundering with a tax lien, he had become someone different than the man she had married. He didn't want to help her with his son, and refused to pay anything – to her or the state. While her head was above water, financially, she was teetering on a fine line that one good bonus or one bad disaster could send her over.

Anne poked Lisa in the arm to get her attention. Lisa snapped to and looked around. Her salon was ready. She almost cried, and when Anne caught her, she turned away laughing. She couldn't help it, this is what Lisa loved. Lisa caught her own reflection in the mirror. She wasn't that fresh face out of cutting school any more. She had grown up, and when did she get old? The tiredness in her feet dragged her body down and she really felt the work she had done today in her back. Lisa crinkled her nose at her reflection and turned away.

"I can't wait to hear what secrets are going to come out of this place," she said. Anne smiled.

"I know. I bet these walls hold more than a few," Anne replied, nodding. "Yours had a couple of stories to tell."

"Oh god, you mean like Jane?"

"Ha, what about Raheleh and Evita?"

"Wow! I forgot all about them."

"You know, that would make for an interesting story."

"We should write a book about it."

So they did.

As the Barber Pole Turns....

When Anne divorced, she had no choice but to take on extra work to pay the bills. She had been generous as an attorney, never caring if clients could not pay. Her practice had a substantial number of pro bono cases. But now she was left with no savings, not realizing until it was too late that her assets were secretly dissipated and the house was under foreclosure. In addition to trying to build a lucrative law practice, she started teaching graduate classes in special education law and took on educational Surrogate work through the State Department of Education. As the divorce drama unfolded, Anne spent many afternoons sitting in front of her computer unable to function. Anne felt betrayed by a man she trusted for close to 29 years; the floor had pretty much opened up and hell was sucking her in.

Simultaneously, Ieva's health deteriorated due to the late onset of Diabetes type one. While trying to stabilize her daughter, Anne was often put into the position of trying to run her law practice from the hospital. As her ex made his grand exit, Anne found creative ways to save a few dollars. She took on a tenant who lived in the room formerly occupied by the nannies. Instead of frequenting high end restaurants, she grew patio tomatoes and raised chickens so the family could enjoy fresh eggs. Eventually she managed to prop her house back on its financial legs with the help of a federal program designed to rescue sinking home owners. She announced to the children that "childhood was over" and her three boys pitched in to do all the "manly" chores around the house in addition to their paid jobs. Her ex never really did go back to work, citing health issues. Anne continues to work long hours. Anne and the 4 children live together, with a cat, dog, and 9 chickens.

When Lisa moved into Jacob's Barbershop, she would start the day the same way Orv did - by turning on the barber pole to let people know that she was open. It was difficult to manage as a single mother so Lisa continues to live in a small apartment almost an hour from New Canaan. Eventually tired of the seven day, one hour commute, she opened up a shop in nearby Southbury as well – with a line of organic products that would hopefully appeal to the clientele that shopped at the organic market next to her new place.

Over time, it was clear that running a shop in Southbury part time was not working out financially. Lisa was not there every day to oversee the shenanigans of the hair dressers, which could be the

subject of another book. She was unable to find someone to buy the Southbury Salon, so she runs the shop at a substantial loss. Lisa is currently paying off high interest credit card bills reflecting what was invested into that business. Lisa was emotionally unable to put the CLOSED sign on the New Canaan door so she now manages 2 shops.

The barber pole continues to turn.

SO YOU'RE THINKING ABOUT CUTTING HAIR? KNOW YOUR STUFF.

There's a lot more to cutting hair than just having a shop and cutting hair. Do you know the difference between a hairstylist and a barber? While both professions deal with cutting hair, a barber is primarily concerned with cutting and styling men's hair. A hairdresser is more concerned with changing or maintaining the image of a person by cutting or styling the person's hair – regardless of gender. They both however, require extensive training and are still very much in demand.

At least once in your life you must have wondered who did some male celebrities' hair that made them look very appealing. You must have looked twice at a billboard because of a celebrity's haircut or you must have once told your barber that you want your haircut like a certain celebrity. Well, you should know that those celebrities must have hired the best barbers there are. These popular celebrity barbers have given impressive haircuts not just to actors but also to athletes, famous businessmen, and other public figures.

A barber is primarily tasked to cut men's hair and shave them if necessary. He is also able to shampoo and style the hair, color it, bleach or even apply highlights to it depending on what his clients would want and what would look best on them. He is focused on making the simplest and traditional short hair styles and he also styles facial hair.

A barber's tools include hair scissors, shaving razors, barber chair, electric hair clipper, barber cloth, comb, hair blower, barber spray, shaving brush, shaving cream, shaving foam, shaving oil, shaving gel, hair cream and a lot more that are needed to perform simple or traditional haircuts and facial hair styling.

If some celebrity hair styles have made you look twice, blame it on their hairdressers. As defined in most dictionaries, a hairdresser isn't just concerned with a person's haircut. Instead, he or she is primarily tasked to maintain or change the image of a person through hair cutting, hair styling, hair coloring, etc. Hairdressers should be talented enough to create different images for their clients and they should also be very good listeners to make sure that they are able to provide exactly what their clients would like. Among the most talented hairdressers are those that provide services to celebrities. They are able to make even the youngest celebrities look old when their roles require it and they are able to make good-looking celebrities look really bad when they need to portray bad roles.

Unlike a barber whose tools are limited to haircutting and facial hair styling needs, a hairdresser would need a lot more than those to be able to perform their tasks. They would need curlers, hair coloring materials, hair texturing materials and a lot more.

What steps should I take to become a barber or a hairdresser?
There are a couple of important steps that you need to take to join the world of hair. You can't just decide that you're going to be a barber – even if you think you are king of the chair. You've got to get the right credentials, such as a barber degree or hairdressing school, and a license to practice what you've learned. Here's a breakdown of the steps needed.

Getting Educated:
If you are really interested in becoming a barber or a hairdresser, you will first need to obtain an education. You will need to have at least a high school diploma to start with – most vocational programs require that to enroll. Unlike attending a four

year college, in hairdressing school, you will only learn the ins and outs of hair, hair cutting, and hair care. Related services are also taught in barber school, such as skin care and scalp care – since most salons and barber shops offer shampoos and shaves.

The vocational program may take up to nine months or longer, depending on whether you are learning to just be a barber, or if you're interested in being a hairdresser. You will want to join an accredited, state-approved cosmetology program. Once you've completed the program, it's important to start compiling a portfolio for future employment needs.

Getting your license:

Again, becoming a barber isn't as easy as going to school and then starting work. Once you've gotten your diploma from a barbering or haircutting school, you'll need to get a license to work – this comes from the state that you live in (or intend to practice haircutting in) and varies from state to state. The most common requirements are:

- being at least 16 years old
- having a high school diploma
- certification that you've completed your courses in barbering college
- certification that you've passed any and all health exams given as required by the state
- Once you've gotten your license and all of your accreditations, you should start looking for employment from reputable salons, spas, hotels and other places where those kinds of services are needed. Also, be aware that as the years pass, styles will change – and this means diligence on the job and constant education.

SIX TIPS FOR BEING A SUCCESSFUL BARBER OR HAIRDRESSER

Hairdressing and barbering is a lucrative job that many people enjoy. It pays well and there is always a need for professionals to cut and style hair. Unfortunately, the licensing and experience aren't the only things that make a hair professional successful – there is also a moral code and set of standards that most hairdressers and barbers strongly live by. Let's take an inside look at some of the other things that make professional hairdressers successful.

- **Be creative.** A barber or hairdresser needs to be with the times – and how to suit whoever sits down in their chair. Creativity helps the barber stay in trend with the times and cope with constant style changing. It also means that they would never run out of styles for their clients to get bored with.

- **Bone up the customer service skills.** Loyalty in the world of hair is indeed everything – a look at the relationship between Anne and Lisa could have told you that. However it's more than loyalty. Relationships have to start somewhere. Relationships begin with a hairdresser or a barber that a client can trust for a fast and accurate haircut that won't leave them feeling disgruntled when they leave the chair.

- **Be a good listener.** Let's face it, there's nothing to do when you're in the salon chair except talk. That isn't the kind of listening that a hair client needs though. Sometimes the client doesn't know what they want and it is the hairdresser's job to satisfy that unnamed need. Pay attention to their details.

- **Be able.** One of the most difficult parts of a hairdressing job for the barber is standing on their feet all day. You must have the stamina to stand, and also your hands must be in good condition so that you can cut, wash, comb and style someone's hair.

- **Keep clean.** This is important. Keeping clean obviously applies to someone's area in the salon, but it also means your personal appearance. It stands to reason that someone who dresses poorly or has sloppy hair themselves could not be trusted to "make someone else look fabulous."

- **Stay focused.** Sometimes being a hairdresser means that you're going to be breaking down a hair job into several steps – occasionally someone will want a color which is a timed process; sometimes, people will need to go under the hair dryer and this is also a timed process. In cases where you're in Hairdressing Hell, you may have to switch between clients because you're the only one in the salon. As Lisa shows us in *Small Town Salon Secrets,* you need to be on your toes when it comes to these procedures. Bad hair = bad money.

Barbers and hairdressers are in demand and it's not just in the United States – people get haircuts all over the world and fresh new fashion is hard to come by. Are you ready?

New Canaan, in Fairfield County, Connecticut

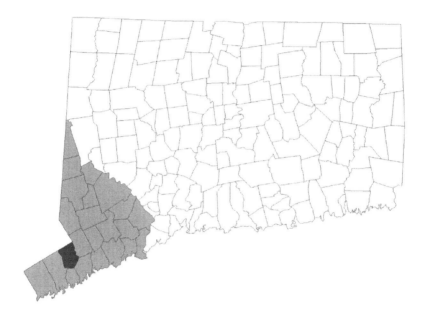

This image has been released into the public domain by its author, VulcanTrekkie45 at the wikipedia project.

Made in the USA
Middletown, DE
13 June 2015